THE INSIDE STORY OF WRESTLING
YOU GRUNT, I'LL GROAN

THE INSIDE STORY OF WRESTLING
YOU GRUNT, I'LL GROAN

Jackie 'Mr TV' Pallo

Macdonald
Queen Anne Press

A Queen Anne Press BOOK

© John Austin 1985

First published in 1985 by
Queen Anne Press, a division of
Macdonald & Co (Publishers) Ltd
Maxwell House, 74 Worship Street
London EC2A 2EN

A BPCC plc Company

All rights reserved. No part of this publication may be reproduced, stored in a retrieval system, or transmitted, in any form or by any means, without the prior permission in writing of the publisher, nor be otherwise circulated in any form of binding or cover other than that in which it is published and without a similar condition including this condition being imposed on the subsequent publisher.

British Library Cataloguing in Publication Data
Pallo, Jackie
　Inside wrestling.
　1. Wrestling—Great Britain—History
　I. Title
　796.8'12'0924　　GV1198.43.A2

ISBN 0-356-10538-5

Typeset by Sunrise Setting, Torquay, Devon

Printed and bound in Great Britain by
Hazell, Watson and Viney Limited
Member of the BPCC Group
Aylesbury, Bucks

CONTENTS

1	The Six Commandments	7
2	The Office Hold	13
3	Come Rassling	33
4	Niggly and Nutty	41
5	Deep Heat and Witchy Poo	46
6	Thwacks, Grunts, Groans and Gutteridge	60
7	The New Boy	72
8	Just Call Me 'Mr TV'	85
9	The Godfather	106
10	Plenty of Seats – Not Enough Arses	117
	Index	125

ONE

THE SIX COMMANDMENTS

We were all at Wembley, waiting for the show to begin. The television camera crews were making last-minute checks, and Kent Walton was brushing up his adjectives. The referee had already been fitted up with the tiny microphone which enabled viewers at home to hear him rasping: 'Stand back! One . . . ah . . . two . . . ah . . . three . . . ah' and so on, and now he was in the dressing room giving out instructions on who was going to win each bout, and when.

'All right, Jackie, go over with a fall in the second and a submission in the third. O.K?' To 'go over' means to win.

The referee was just rounding off his spiel when the door flew open, and a man rushed in, wide-eyed, pulled him aside, and whipped off his microphone.

'The bloody mike is live,' he hissed. 'The camera crew heard everything you said.' Oh dear, oh dear! Panic. But what to do? 'I'll pretend it was a joke,' says the ref, and we all grin and chuckle while he says things like: 'That got you going didn't it. Fooled you all, eh? Ho ho.'

Then he did a quick re-shuffle of the script, with different results in different rounds, so that the cameramen, hopefully, would be convinced everything was above board.

Hilarious, really, but it also shows how desperate we all were to protect the name of our game, the image, the great illusion, the belief of several million faithful fans that professional wrestling is a straight, competitive sport in which the best man wins. All nonsense, of course, but everybody in the game is brainwashed into believing that it will die if the punters ever suspect that it is all a fake: that wrestlers are not superhuman characters, strong enough to endure much more pain than other men. That the blood, the groans, the screams of rage and pain, the twisted limbs and lethal knockout moves are designed to entertain them, so they'll keep paying at the door to put their arses on seats.

Of course, plenty of people have pointed the finger and shouted 'phoney' over the years, but the fanatical punters remained convinced, and faithful, and there were plenty more who weren't quite sure, but enjoyed the spectacle. Plus the bar-room bores who natter on about some fights being fixed, just like in boxing, but that anybody with half an eye could easily tell a genuine match from a faked one.

All garbage, but what did it matter as long as the game flourished and made a lot of money? Which it would continue to do as long as there were no leaks from *inside*, especially from very big established names, like me.

Indeed, I've been conditioned for so many years by the wrestling Mafia's '*omerta*' rule of silence, that I already feel a touch uneasy. A lot of people will be upset, some of them nastily, and several million fans will not thank me for disillusioning them.

Nevertheless, it has to be said that so far as I'm concerned most pro wrestling is bent, bogus, moody, sham, make believe and all my eye. In nearly 35 years I can hardly remember fighting a straight fight, and I have seldom heard of a straight pro fight.

Wrestling is a branch of showbusiness. And just as Jack never really hurts the giant at the top of the beanstalk, the goodies and baddies of wrestling — we call them 'villains' and 'blue-eyes' — seldom give each other pain, unless it is by accident. Believe me, that's just about the only way anyone gets hurt. How else do you think that wrestlers can carry on fighting, four, sometimes five times a week when they are past the age of 60? In September 1983, aged 58, I had a great bout despite being almost crippled by two extremely painful arthritic hips. One has since been replaced, and the other will be operated upon shortly. Stand by: I may make a comeback!

'Ah yes,' the bar-room pundits will say, 'but it's a different story when somebody loses his temper, isn't it? What about when so-and-so went berserk and knocked you cold?' More cobblers. Going off his rocker was all part of his act. I've never known him really lose his temper.

Many times, punters have come up to me after a show and said: 'What a fight Jackie. You could certainly tell that was for real.' Naturally, I agreed with them. It was my job. And if anybody points the finger, close ranks. We certainly did that.

The other day I found a pile of old newspaper cuttings in which I, and a bundle of other wrestlers, am quoted getting quite heated over the mere suggestion that the game could be hocus-pocus.

'What do you mean, a carve up?' I demanded of one reporter. 'It's a slander. We get badly hurt.' To later questions I indignantly pointed out that wrestlers could be put out of action for a month, even a year, with broken joints, or torn ligaments.

At these times, I remembered the grunt and groan commandments which the great old-timers, solemnly drummed into me, over and over:

— Thou shalt not talk to strangers about the game, or discuss it within their hearing, especially in pubs or cafés.
— Thou shalt not invite, or allow, strangers to enter the dressing room, however important they may be.
— Thou shalt not tell any member of the public what you earn for a fight. (This was because they didn't want people to know our money was so pathetically poor.)
— Thou shalt never reveal to punters the dates and places at which you are scheduled to appear. (This was because pros who fight each other regularly tend to stick to the same pattern when they are appearing in towns far apart, but promoters want the public to think wrestlers meet each other only infrequently. So it wouldn't do if a keen bunch of punters got to know where you were due to fight, followed you from town to town, and realised that the act was always the same.)
— Thou shalt always protect the game.

Well, I've protected the game for a long time, and I'd have carried on doing it if the promoters' commitment to the most important commandment of them all — Thou shalt always endeavour to give the punters good value for their money — wasn't heading for the scrap-heap.

The punters are entitled to be entertained by a skilled, showmanlike or flamboyant performance which is at least capable of belief. Instead, more and more, they are being

THE SIX COMMANDMENTS

subjected to a mis-matched shambles which relies heavily on gimmicks and what I believe to be the downright grotesque.

I mean, how many times can a punter be expected to pay to watch two overweight lummoxes bump stomachs and belly flop for maybe three, or perhaps five minutes if they are feeling particularly fit and generous? Incredibly, this sort of thing can still attract six-and-a-half million viewers on ITV's 'World of Sport' every Saturday — a programme on which I have been seen wrestling many, many times. But, because the standard of the television shows is declining so rapidly, the game is fast dying in the halls. Often they are more than half empty.

The television chiefs *must* have been convinced that pro wrestling was for real, otherwise surely they wouldn't have allowed pro bouts to be shown in the company of really great genuine sporting events? After all, an element of competition is essential if an activity is to be classified as a 'sport', so they couldn't have believed that there wasn't that element in the pro game. If they did, it would have been like screening a local football derby, even though they knew the two teams had decided before kick-off who was going to win, and by how many goals.

Not that I'm complaining. Television made me a big star. I'm simply wondering how long the 'World of Sport' executives can justify screening the present Saturday rubbish and call it sport. At its best, pro wrestling could only be described as a 'sporting spectacle'. That it certainly was. Now it is not.

And it is no longer the game — the business — I once vowed to protect.

My enemies will say that this is all bollocks. They will say that I am writing this for money (correct) because I am bitter over my failure to win a share of the lucrative television wrestling contract. They will say that I am furious because I have been forced out of big time promoting by the wrestling establishment, and because I have lost a lot of money.

They are absolutely right.

I still have the flair to keep the game alive and healthy. I could have tried to cut out the canker that I believe is killing it. I would have given the punters value for money, in the halls and on the box. I am certainly not talking bollocks.

Judge for yourself.

TWO
THE OFFICE HOLD

Ever since the first punter paid good money to watch two wrestlers grunt and groan, the game has been in the grip of a hold which you will never hear anyone discuss — the Office Hold. It's the only hold to which a wrestler must submit every time he fights, if he wants to keep earning that is.

The office decides where, when and who a man will fight, and for how much. Or even whether or not he will be seen fighting on television. Try and break the Office Hold and you can start looking for work elsewhere. I know.

The Office Hold is the script for that night's show which is used to brief the lads on who is to win, in how many rounds, and in which rounds falls, submissions, knockouts or disqualifications will take place. If a bout is said to be 'cats' or 'monkeys', it means that nobody will win, as cat's paw and monkey's paw are rhyming slang for 'draw'.

Now, if the office wants to make money — and it does — it has to put on a good variety show. It is necessary to balance the acts in a way that will please the punters. For instance, the show may start off with a forearm smashing, body slamming bloodbath between two large, fearsome and overweight characters, then follow them, in direct contrast, with two 'shooters' — fast clean-limbed clear-eyed young men, scientific, full of backward somersaults and cartwheels, who frequently shake hands and help each other up. This gives punters the opportunity to nod wisely and chunter on about how it is a nice change to see clean wrestling and good sportsmanship, unlike the carryings on of that dirty swine Pallo, who'll be on next. But as soon as they've said that they begin to get bored, so these bouts usually don't last long. Enter the villain, snarling and sneering at the crowd, breaking every rule (what rules?) in the book, while his opponent blue-eye, who is everybody's ideal husband, lover, son, valiantly tries to play it clean. When, for a moment, he finally loses control and lashes back at the villain, he is ticked off by the referee, for gawd's sake, while the other bugger has been

THE OFFICE HOLD

getting away with murder. It's hard to believe, isn't it?

Lovely. This creates heat, emotion, and gives everyone a chance to jump up and down, screaming and bawling and working off their frustrations and inhibitions. Sometimes they get carried away and try to kill the villain, which is bad news.

After all the screaming, a lot of the punters will be hoarse, and feeling a bit limp, so that quite a few could be wandering out when the M.C. asks you to give a big hand to two up-and-coming youngsters who have travelled 200 miles, all the way from Aberdeen, to entertain them, etc. They will close the show.

Women have whispered to me that they get a sexual kick watching well-muscled, sweaty bodies writhing about in the ring. Others confessed they loved villains because 'you're so dominant', but most seem to cast baddies in the role of the boss, husband, or some other man they hate, while blue-eye is the lover, or son, or husband (if they like him) who will give him his comeuppance. Forget Freud, just quote Pallo.

To help him vary the mix the matchmaker can call upon masked fighters, and characters who are supposed to be cowboys, bullfighters, Red Indian braves, butlers, African chiefs, massive Chinese, enormous Japanese, disgraced doctors, titanic Turks, phoney peers of the realm, and the rest of the United Nations, as well as blokes who are 'experts' at karate, judo, and every other martial art. As a special treat, he might match two good villains, like Mick McManus and myself, so that the punters could have a good time trying to decide which one they hate most.

McManus, incidentally, was one of promoter Dale Martin's matchmakers for some time. All the lads called him 'Paramount' because they reckoned all his bills were like a mountain with a star on top, just like the film company's trade mark. Our Mick, of course, was the star, and the mountain was the supporting cast. Nevertheless, whether it was single combat or tag (pairs) wrestling, Mick generally stuck to the well-tried formula of good versus evil, like in western films and pantomime, the only difference being that good frequently did not triumph. Villains like me, McManus and Steve Logan were always winning. We were good showmen who pulled the crowds.

If I'd lost nearly every time, people would soon have stopped coming to see me. But when I kept winning they had to come back again, hoping to see me thrashed, but not being too disappointed if I cheated yet another good man of victory with my nasty, diabolical tricks. I knew I'd done my job well if the punters wandered away muttering: 'I don't know how that bastard Pallo manages to get away with it. He was bloody lucky again tonight. Next time . . . ' The operative word was 'lucky'. And if I had to lose, then I lost well, often on a technicality. Maybe I'd be having a steaming ruck with a punter and the referee would count me out because I had one leg the wrong side of the ropes. I'd be 'unlucky', and the punters would say: 'I know that Pallo's a shit, but you must admit he was unlucky to lose that one. Next time . . . '

Yes, and next time I wrestled, they'd be there again, *paying to put their arses on seats*. And that is what it is all about.

A wrestling punter expects full value for money, in terms of time, if he is going to keep on buying tickets. If he went to watch boxing and saw four fighters knocked out in the first half minute of the first round in each bout, he'd be talking about the spectacular evening he'd had for ages. But if the same thing happened when he went to his local swimming baths to watch wrestling, he'd likely join the rest of the mob in tearing the ring apart. Pro punters expect their bouts to last between 20 and 35 minutes, and only expect to think about going home at about 10 p.m. to 10.30 p.m. It does not seem to occur to the fanatical that there may be something odd about the convenience of this arrangement. Those who do think about it don't care as long as they enjoy themselves.

At a good show the punter is never allowed to become bored, and this is where matchmaking is so important. For instance, it is no good pitting two technically excellent wrestlers — 'shooters' — against each other unless one of them is an extrovert. And shooters who are also good showmen are very thin on the ground. The trouble with brilliant wrestlers is that most of them are egoists and always want to win. Since they can't both win, you usually end up with a move for move, spoiling fight, in which there is no give and take and which is only of interest to other wrestlers. Eyelids begin to droop, and as far as the punters are concerned it is a 'pony' (bad, or boring) bout.

Also, too many shooters fail to understand that the average pro punter knows little about the finer points of the real sport of wrestling, and is therefore unable to appreciate how good they are. Sometimes two top shooters will wrestle for real for a couple of rounds to prove who is the better man. When that happens the observant punter will notice that all the other wrestlers come out to watch.

For instance, if you put Jack Dempsey and Cliff Beaumont in the ring together, the crowd would probably take forty winks if they weren't catcalling. There would be no spark, no heat. But put me in with either of them, and we'd have a great fight. They'd provide the wrestling, and I'd throw myself all over the place to provide the spectacle.

Many superb wrestlers had no punter-pulling appeal as individuals, and, when mis-matched, often died the death. Even men like Eric Sands, Eric Taylor, Billy Joyce, Ernie Baldwin, Brian Maxine, and Billy Robinson, king of the British heavyweights, who finally went to America because he got fed up earning peanuts here. I stayed with Billy once, when I was a novice, and I was trying to get to sleep in the spare room when Billy let his bulldog in to share it with me. The hound jumped onto the bed and lay down with his whacking great head just a foot from my own. Bear in mind, a week later, the same bloody dog went straight through the plate glass window of Billy's mother's hairdressing shop in Manchester to get at a cat. He growled like he was hungry, all night, even when he was dozing, and I was afraid to move in case he ended up with my head tucked underneath his paw. Billy was grinning all over his face when he looked in next morning. 'Sleep well?' he said.

Years later we were getting into our gear in the dressing room at Liverpool, when I saw Billy put on a pair of striped shorts, like mine. I was the only wrestler using striped shorts at the time. It was my first trademark, and I thought this would never do. 'You realise, Billy,' I said, 'that by wearing those shorts you become a clown like me?' He looked hard at me, then stripped off the shorts, handed them to me and said: 'Keep 'em.'

Billy was one of a number of fighters who would never allow himself to be defeated unless he was convinced that man was capable of beating him. I remember a fighter appearing to take on Billy. The man had been on television that afternoon, and he chuntered on about how he should go over because wasn't he the TV star? Billy disagreed. Television did not impress him. He must have scraped the poor bloke over every inch of the groin (wrestling ring) that night. A really gentle gentleman outside the ring, is Billy. But he could be a bit vicious inside it.

I had the same problem with a German who came over to wrestle me in Wales. When he was told that I was to go over (win), he said: 'Nein, nein, last night I on television was'. I said: 'Listen mate, in this country I'm Mr TV and I'm going over.' But when we got in the groin it was obvious he intended to change the script. I tried throwing him about a bit, but found he was a much better wrestler than me and there was no way I was going to win. So I chinned him and knocked him out. All dramatic stuff. The referee pointed to the corner and I was disqualified amongst much ranting and finger waving. It didn't matter. Everyone, particularly the German, knew who was guv'nor, and that was what counted. Afterwards we shook hands. There's rarely much grudge-holding in the pro game. Occasionally a couple of shooters will go down to the gym to prove which one is boss, but pros without wrestling egos, like me, ignore that and concentrate on getting as much money as we can for the next fight.

Among the wrestlers who took their pride seriously are Bert Asseratti and Les Kellett, fighters of the old school, when men used to knock each other about a lot more in the groin. They were heavy (serious wrestlers). I remember Bert coming into the dressing room, leering at Tibor Szakacs and saying:

THE OFFICE HOLD

'You're a nice piece of white meat, eh, Tibor?' Meaning that he'd like to get the Hungarian into the groin and bounce him all around it. Tibor, who could be a bit heavy himself, did not look too happy. Bert got a bit like that one night – I believe at Aberdeen — when he was up against Mike Marino, billed as Golden Boy (we called him Golden Bollocks). Mike was prancing around, playing the golden champ, and this prompted Bert to teach him a lesson. Whack! Mike ended up with the finest pair of cauliflower ears I've ever seen and had concussion for about a week. As for Les, he's probably the hardest man in wrestling today. Not a man to mix it with. When he hits you around the face with one of his slaps, it's grit your teeth time. I once asked Les if he knew of a way to produce blood from an opponent without doing too much damage, as the punters love a bit of claret. 'Just keep bashing them hard on the nose,' he said.

Now, I've never refused to lose to a man, because I regarded the game as showbiz, and I was there to entertain. So I'd rather have a marvellous bout and lose than a pony bout and win. On the other hand, there were many shooters who wouldn't agree to lie down for me. In a real shoot, many of these could have beaten me sitting in a wheelchair using one hand. But, as I've said, real wrestling is seldom entertaining as a spectator sport. There were exceptions, of course. I never won against the incomparable George Kidd. Who did? George wouldn't take a dive for anyone.

I think I was the first lightweight to top bills, but George was the greatest lightweight of all time, a one off, a tremendous performer who had a distinctive style that no one could possibly copy. He was faster than a twinkle in the eye, and his escape moves were sheer magic. But George always made me look good while I lost. In other words, like me, he felt it was best to arrange to beat someone without destroying or humiliating them. Sometimes, a man would say to me: 'Look, Jackie, we'll be fighting in my home town. How about letting me go over?' I'd tell him no, I couldn't do that, but I'd give him a bloody good bout, make him look really good.

As a blue-eye, George was dazzling, and he had good

company in Steve Vidor, the boy every bird and mummy loved to love, and Vic Faulkner and his brother, Bert Royal, who was whiter than white. When I wrestled Bert at Leicester Baths a black wreath from the punters was handed to me in the ring. Charming.

Also, Bert and Vic were easily the biggest draw as a goody tag team. Among the major baddies facing them were myself, Alan Colbeck (with whom I tagged for a time), Steve Logan, Chick Purvey (a great grafter) and Mick McManus.

For a blue-eye versus villain bout to get the punters really heated up, there has to be close co-operation, connivance, and understanding between the opponents. There must be give and take, with the fortunes of good and evil seesawing back and fore until one finally triumphs. Timing has to be good. If you let a man get out of a good hold too quickly, it becomes meaningless. But equally, if you keep the hold on too long, it becomes boring. Also it is important for fighters to respond to each other's moves. For example, if I'd just dropped a man on his head with a fucking great bang, I'd expect him to roll around on the deck for some seconds, clutching his nut as if in agony. This is called 'dying' to the other man's move, or 'selling' his move. One problem with Bert Royal and Vic Faulkner was that you had to die to their moves, because people loved them, but they were most reluctant to die to yours. I'd give Bert (or Vic) a whack that would have kept McManus groaning on the deck for a while, and he would pop back up, like a jack-in-the-box, as if I'd hit him with a feather, and thump me with his elbow. To make them respond you had to hit them with a four pound hammer. Not only that, but they went on a bit. One drop kick was not good enough for Bert or Vic. You had to take three in a row. It made everything hard, and by the time I left the ring I'd be panting like a 90 fags a day man. And that's not good for you.

Ideally, every bout should tell a little tale. Perhaps I would build up a story around my opponent's left arm, which would be heavily bandaged at the elbow. I'd keep attacking it, jerking it hard, then jeer at him, and the punters, while he hopped around nursing it, cursing and looking daggers. For variation, I'd switch now and again to the other arm, but always returning to the one I was weakening in preparation for the submission or fall.

'He's working on that weak arm again,' Kent Walton would say sadly. 'I don't know how much more of that Royal can take.' Any amount: it wasn't hurting him nearly as much as he pretended.

Normally, I like to wrestle straight for a short while from the off, letting my opponent make the moves, while I escape and look clever and arrogant. Then I'd start to take over and, maybe, get him to the deck and stand over him, so he couldn't get up. That always gees up the crowd. Or perhaps I'd drag him off the floor, which is 'illegal', throw him about a bit, use the elbow, and be generally dastardly. Then just as it looked as if it was all over for him, he'd make a comeback and I'd be in all sorts of trouble. 'Take me leg, throw me off the ropes. Chin me,' I'd whisper. The crowd loved it, and as soon as they were up, ranting, I'd mutter: 'Die again, die. Leave it to me. Bring 'em down,' and you could almost hear the punters collectively groaning: 'Gawd, the bastard's got him again.'

Always I could gauge the reaction of the crowd, sense the extent of its heat, and I'd instinctively know when to take a fall, or give one. When I became a big star, I could get away with a lot of things. I played to the mood of the punters and, because I was a huge draw, I had the power to get away with it.

Unhappily, my increasing fame fostered growing jealousy and resentment in other wrestlers, particularly when northern boys came south to wrestle, and vice versa. Needle crept in — some of it encouraged by the promoters because they thought it good for the show — and I had trouble several times in the north, especially with one lad, a much better wrestler than me, which he obviously knew. He wouldn't sell any of my moves, so I wouldn't die to any of his. A lot of niggle crept in. I was on the brink of putting one on him, and maybe he realised it, because he decided to let me go over, though with very bad grace.

I have heard some pundits claim that every fight is carefully rehearsed in the gym, move by move, before being presented in public. This is utter nonsense. So are the claims that fighters get a bonus if they win. They don't. The money is the same, win or lose. Neither do they talk to each other in 'code' in the groin (unless cockney rhyming slang can be interpreted as code); nor do they pretend to be badly hurt to 'fool' their opponents.

If I was about to start on a series of fights with another good pro, I'd just get together with him and we'd discuss how to play it. I'd say something like: 'Right, I'll take a fall in the second, you take one in the fourth, and I'll finish with my usual back submission in the fifth.' I wouldn't have to tell him what my usual back submission was. He'd know. He'd also be well aware of my fighting style, and if we were both on the same wavelength as far as the audience was concerned, we'd have a great tour. As for the falls, I'd talk him through the fight and play it by ear on the first night. After that, the action would remain basically the same, night after night, like a cabaret act, though we might introduce a new move from time to time for the sake of variation. When I was fighting another good pro, it was normal for him to be awarded a fall, or submission for the sake of his reputation, and to give the punters their money's worth. But with a lesser man, or a relative novice, I would try to win with two quick falls to emphasise my superiority as the star, and the M.C. would ask the crowd to give a big hand to the brave and promising youngster who had come such a cropper.

In the pro game everything has to be greatly exaggerated, much larger than life — just like pantomime. And to achieve this it is necessary to supplement the genuine amateur moves and holds — known as 'shoot moves' — with spectacular gimmick moves and holds, which are bugger all to do with the true sport, but are purely to entertain the punter.

These are called 'working moves', and hundreds of them have been invented by enterprising showmen — 'grafters' — like myself, over the past 40 years. Inside the game a fighter was identified by his speciality working move in much the same way as a clown owned the copyright on his 'face', and it was not considered healthy to steal another man's move. Big

Daddy and Giant Haystacks are, presumably, identified by their bellies.

Many of these working moves rely considerably on the co-operation of a wrestler's opponent. He has to let you put on the hold (often seeming to be dazed at the time) or he has actively to help you to put it on. For example, it is virtually impossible to Irish Whip a man unless he obliges by jumping up and turning a somersault for you. The same thing applies to the Flying Head Scissors, and Flying Head Mare, the Monkey Climb, Grapevine and many others. However, most moves, whether shoot or working, are potentially dangerous and some could be lethal. So there is not too much margin for error. That's where the professionalism comes in.

Cliff Beaumont had a terrific throw. He'd get my head between his thighs, then put his arms around my legs and heave up, at the same time releasing my head. If he did it properly, I'd flip right over and land on my feet. It looked great. However, if his timing was a little off, you landed on your back, and it bloody well hurt. That sort of throw could have a really nasty result if some novice tried to copy it in a cowboy show.

Bert Royal used to specialise in the Indian Death Lock, which you cannot put on unless everything is in the right place. When Bert leaned right back, his opponent would start banging the deck and screaming submission. Bert would only have to get one small thing wrong, and the man would be *really* screaming. As a tag team, the Royals invented a fast, exciting move, criss-crossing the ring at speed, bouncing off the ropes and diving through the legs (or over the top) of befuddled opponents before going for the kill. It was called Criss Cross Quiz, or Cross Country.

Top grafters would work out a move and then practise it in the gym. I remember, when I was a novice, George Kidd showing me in the dressing room at Poole a move he'd been working on. One of the lads lay on the floor, face down, and George quickly put his feet at the back of the bloke's knees, leaned forward and caught hold of his arms, then threw himself backwards. George ended up on his back with the other bloke suspended above him, staring at the ceiling. He said it took him a long time to get it right, as he had to do it entirely on his own.

Ricki Starr used to do an Aeroplane Spin, followed by a body slam, and when you reached the deck you really were giddy. Johnny Czeslaw would bounce through the ropes, out of the ring, about four times a bout. It was tiring to watch him. Tibor Szakacs was noted for his chops to the chest. Now when you chop you turn your hand at the last second, so that it is the flat of the hand which connects, not the edge. He used to hit so hard he'd leave a hand print showing on your chest, and it hurt. I used to tell the silly bugger off about it.

'Karate' chops to the throat ended up with the palm of the hand thwacking the chest underneath the throat. Let's not be stupid. If a big man genuinely hit you very hard on your windpipe with the edge of his hand, you'd more than likely be pushing up daisies in a couple of days.

When I was tagging with Alan Colbeck, one of the routines was for him to Head Mare my man in front of the post, then for me to climb quickly to the top of the post and jump off it, landing with my knee across his throat. He would go into convulsions, and so would the ladies at the ringside. Everybody would be happy. But if my knee had hit his throat, with my weight and the impetus of my jump from the post behind it, the poor lad would have ended up on a slab. Mind you, the timing has to be perfect for that one. Another time I tried the move and my opponent chickened out at the last second and moved as I was on the way down. There's a man with no conscience!

Another wrestler specialises in left-handed Forearm Smashes, but his forearms actually smack the flesh at the top of the chest. It is the other man jerking his head back that makes it look realistic. When I put my foot on an opponent's nose and spin around on it, I apply no pressure with that foot at all. I'm pivoting on the other foot, and it supports all my weight. When I stomp on, or kick a man on the deck, my boot scarcely touches him. I jump up with the other foot at the same time, and it is that foot which makes the satisfyingly

THE OFFICE HOLD

damaging noise. If I drop a wrestler onto my knee, my foot is still off the ground when I *place* him on it. When he touches my knee, I bend my leg, angle my knee so it faces downwards, and let him slide off it.

Bert Asseratti favoured the Boston Crab. Now, when you've got a fighter flat on his face and you've got his feet under your arms, with your back to him, and his knees are off the floor, there's no way he can escape. If you leaned right back then, he'd scream so loud the light bulbs would shatter. Of course you don't, because it would be stupid. Bert expected his opponent to submit straight away when he applied the Crab. If they didn't, he might give them a touch of agony just to teach them a lesson. It was his gentle way. Nowadays, however, the victim of a Boston Crab frequently does a quick press up and propels the other bloke arse over tip with his legs. It looks good, yes, and usually gets a cheer. But it's virtually impossible without collaboration.

So is the Body Slam. Obviously, if an eighteen stone man was really slammed onto his back from about six feet up, his wife would either be calling at the morgue to identify him, or visiting him in hospital for umpteen years. What happens is that the attacker gets his man in a crutch hold, and the geezer pushes off with his toes to help with the lift. Now he's up there, upside down, and the slammer makes sure the man's body is perfectly straight before smashing him hard onto the deck *at an angle*, so that the full impact is taken on the heels of his boots, and his body only has a few inches to fall. It doesn't hurt at all — done properly. Similarly, with a Backbreaker, you actually support the man's weight at both ends, and as for drop kicks, you've got to walk into them, then throw yourself backwards, to make them look effective. Let's face it, if you tried a dropkick in a real fight, the bloke would simply step to one side and watch you bounce on your butt, as he'd have to be in a coma not to see it coming.

Postings are another bit of nonsense. Watch closely and you can see the man running backwards into them. In any case they are padded. 'Oh dear,' says Kent Walton, 'that's his third Posting, and he's looking pretty hurt and shaky.'

Actually, promoters don't like Postings because they can damage the ring. Neither do they like very heavy men being Body Slammed. It tends to crack the boards.

Quite a few moves don't have any name at all. Sometimes Kent will think one up. I believe Stepover Toehold was one of his. Nifty, eh? I could go on about Figure Fours, the Shortarm Scissors, the Victory Roll, Head Butts, Flying Tackles, Arm Jerks, Body Checks, and whatever. But I think I've said enough to make it clear that if everything in the game was as it seems, fights would last minutes, or even seconds, and every night joints would crack, tendons snap, bones break, shoulders dislocate, necks loll, and several good men would be promoted to the great groin in the sky.

I was noted for contriving to run into the top rope, when I'd spin right over and be left hanging with my neck caught between two ropes, my eyes bulging and making choking sounds. Punters would crowd around to release my head and there'd be lots of fuss and people asking if I was all right. I'd rub my neck, totter around a bit, and bravely carry on.

One night this trick was nearly my undoing. Two punters jumped up and heaved on my legs to try to pull my head free. This cut off my air and I didn't have to do any acting at all.

Another stunt was to arrange for myself to be thrown out of the ring. I used to vary these falls quite a lot. Sometimes I'd go feet first, other times head first; sometimes I'd be face down, other times face up. I'd go over the top rope, through the ropes, or under them. Always I'd catch a rope while going out, so that I hit the deck with my feet before hitting the floor, making a big bang with one hand and, perhaps, sweeping some chairs over with the other. Once, I crashed out of the ring and knocked over several cameras and Kent Walton in full spiel. I didn't hurt him, because I knew what I was doing. I believe he carried on talking. He's a hard man to silence, that one. It all looked, and sounded, ever so painful, and I'd either stay out, pretending to be unconscious or badly hurt, or stagger back into the ring only just in time to beat the count. This to make it convincing for the punters.

I'd also take a run at a geezer and do a dropkick. When he

stepped out of the way I'd catch my legs on the top rope and pretend it had caught my goolies. All the breaths being sucked in nearly created a vacuum. Women put their hands to their mouths. Men went white, screwed up their eyes and put their hands in their pockets. I clutched my crutch and made like the Inquisition was doing a job on me. All very effective. When I first did it, another wrestler came up to me a few days later and said: 'How's your balls? You didn't half give them a whack the other night.' And when another wrestler says that, you know you've been good.

One of my specialities was the Back Arm Submission. I'd lift my man off the ground, holding both his arms up behind his back. He'd push up with his feet at the same time, and I'd lean back and support his weight while he hollered that he wanted to give in.

I was also the first wrestler in Britain to do Head Drops. I'd hold my opponent upside down, with his head between my knees, hair hanging down, then wallop! I'd crash down and his head seemed to meet the deck with a bang. Actually, it was my knees that made the bang, as his head was an inch or two from the floor. Sometimes I'd drop from about four feet, and this move did my knees so much mischief that eventually I had to give it up, or risk ending up like Toulouse Lautrec.

A day I really enjoyed was when I fought a televised match with Alan Dennison at the Seymour Hall. As a bonus for the punters, he hit me after the final bell, and I died to the move, falling onto the deck. I could feel my lip was bleeding, and the crowd was baying, so I decided to take advantage of the situation, and stayed down, pretending to be spark out. Seconds and ambulancemen failed to revive me, and I was carried to the dressing room to be attended to by our own 'doctor'. As soon as the door closed, I got up, had a wash and made with the sticking plaster. It was a nasty cut, but nothing too bad, although my lip has sloped to one side ever since. Anyway, later that day they flashed a picture of me on the box, and the news presenter said I'd recovered consciousness in hospital, and was improving. What a lark. Can't imagine who told them.

Talking of accidents, I once ended a round two minutes early by throwing myself over the top rope backwards and landing on the bell with a loud dong. At the last second, the timekeeper moved it to the place I'd chosen to fall on, and this did my back no good. I've hit chairs too, which people have moved to the wrong place just as I launched myself into the air. Add to this the innumerable falls I've taken on my back, and you'll understand why I've made osteopaths rich trying to do something about a dislocated spinal disc which occasionally traps a nerve and makes my left leg go wonky. For, however well you fall on your back, you usually jar the spine a little, even though the ring is normally five-ply wood cushioned with felt. It's still hard, and some rings have less 'give' than others.

My elbow joints are like rusty hinges and won't let me straighten my arms properly. I've used them so many times to break my fall that each one has a big knob on it.

I've strained my ankles more times than I can count. Ditto for broken fingers and ribs, and, twenty years ago I was about to throw an elbow at Jack Cunningham, at Southampton, when I tripped badly and twisted my knee, which ballooned nicely. The rugby-playing doctor at the London Hospital said he wouldn't have the cartilage out if he was me, as I wouldn't be able to wrestle again for a long time if I did. He stuck a very large syringe in the side of my knee, pumped a lot of drug in, and said to keep tensing my muscles when the swelling went down, to help keep the cartilage in place.

This I did, and mostly it stayed put. Now and again it popped out when I was in the groin, and I'd push it back in with my hand. My nose has been bent (mainly by Alan Dennison), my lips split, and I doubt whether there's a tendon or ligament which has escaped unhurt, or a square inch of flesh which hasn't at some time been bruised.

But my worst injury was no accident. I was wrestling a man in a sleazy hall in Paris. Judo Al Hayes and Ray Hunter, were with me, and they were watching the bout from the cine-projector aperture high up on a wall.

Suddenly this man Head Mared me and, while I was still on

the deck, he drew back his boot and kicked me full in the mouth. I got up, spitting blood, and looked at the referee, who said: 'I theenk ees ad a few dreenks'. A few drinks! There were my lovely teeth all fractured, and this berk smiling at me as if he'd done something clever. I looked up and saw Alfie and Ray breaking their ribs laughing, and this didn't help. I hit him as hard as I could with my right, and when he went down I jumped on him and screwed him something rotten. Believe me, there was nothing phoney about his submission. I gave him a lot more stick for two rounds, and he was ever so glad to get back to the dressing room.

Afterwards, Al Hayes offered to buy me a meal to cheer me up. Then he looked at my north and south and said: 'Well, you can keep me company'. I watched him get through a mound of lovely French food while I tried to spoon down some mashed-up tomatoes.

Back in London they discovered I had a broken jaw. My front teeth were all facing backwards, like some monster, and four of them had to be cut from the gums. Now all my front noshers are false. But I'm still the prettiest.

That was, I think, the only fight I ever won for real. Inside the ring, that is. Outside, there were one or two bits of aggro, though very little when you consider it's spread over more than 30 years.

In the early days, I had several punch-ups in the dressing room — one of them with Archie O'Brien, an experienced man who'd been all through the Burma campaign, and, understandably I suppose, was a little irritated by cheeky youngsters like me. Beforehand, in the ring, we were being geed up by an RAF man in the crowd named Frankie Hughes, who became a pro wrestler ten years later. 'You're a couple of old grannies. I'll take on the pair of you,' Frankie shouted. Archie turned, glared and pointed. 'I'll have that man,' he said. It was his favourite saying. Instead, he decided to have me. I was making moves he didn't approve of, and I could see he was furious that the new boy had the nerve to be so daring. It got a bit lippy, and we started swapping punches. The punters must have thought they were in the wrong hall.

Anyway, he went over, with me snarling defiance, and we carried on with our bare knuckle bit in the dressing room. After the bruises healed, we became great pals — as often happens — and I occasionally picked up his boys, Bob and Tony, from school. Years later, I ended up wrestling against them.

At Lime Grove, I had a run-in with an opponent, over something which had not gone right on the night. He took a swing at me and split my ear open. I was doing my best to split him, when Mike Marino separated us, and delivered a little lecture: 'Thou shalt not fight unless thou gets paid.'

In the late sixties, when I was silly big, I had trouble with Abe Ginsberg, at Hanley. We had aggravation in the ring, because I thought he wasn't dying to my stuff, and he thought I was stealing too much of the limelight, which I probably was. We argued in the dressing room, and I was sitting on a chair when he slapped me, hard, across the face. I got up and put him down, and it went on from there. Bert Royal and Vic Faulkner were interested spectators, and two Greek wrestlers, also on the bill, hid behind the coats. Every now and then they popped out their heads, jabbered to each other, and their faces clearly said: 'Look at those two cunts beating hell out of each other when nobody is paying them any money'. When we stopped, we shook hands, and we were very friendly afterwards. But I knew the word would get around, so the following morning, I phoned Wryton Promotions and told them I didn't want Abe losing any work because of our private upset, and that they could bill me against him any time. I had that sort of clout then. For a couple of weeks, Abe made a gag out of it. He went around saying: 'Here, they say that Pallo don't make a comeback,' and rubbing his jaw. What he meant was that I would always take a lot of stick before taking offence.

Indeed, I took a lot before taking offence with Peter Keenan, former bantam-weight boxing champion and world contender, holder of two Lonsdale belts. Or at least J.J. (my son, Jackie Junior) did. I'd just started promoting on my own, and was working with Max Crabtree in opposition to Dale

THE OFFICE HOLD

Martin and company. Keenan was promoting fights in Scotland, and we'd just appeared on one of his bills in Glasgow. We were waiting for our travelling money — the fares — when Max came out of Keenan's office and said he didn't think it would be a good idea if we went in, as Keenan was upset because he'd lost money. Me and J.J. thought this was rubbish and, being young, keen, in the right and in a temper, J.J. went steaming in and started arguing with Keenan. I followed him in.

Without warning, Keenan laid a hook on my chin, and I went staggering back. Next second he floored J.J. with a lovely punch on the point of the chin, and put him spark out.

I put up my hand and did my gentlemanly bit. 'Right,' I said, 'if you want to fight, we'll fight.' I took my watch off, pulled by wallet from my pocket, peeled of my jacket and handed them all to Shirley Crabtree, now known as Big Daddy, who was also on the bill. Then Keenan and I squared up. It didn't last very long, since all my old boxing training came to my aid and I beat him easily. However, we made up the next day. But J.J. and I never got our travelling money.

Since then, J.J. has always kept his chin well tucked in when arguing with somebody who's a bit useful.

Please don't think this kind of thing happened only to me. A lot of people got into whackings.

One night me and J.J. were sitting in the dressing room of a Birmingham hall, together with Kendo Nagasaki, a big, tasty man who was still wearing his mask, and Peter Preston, a good, hard little wrestler who lacks charisma. Nagasaki was sitting in the armchair, but when he went out for a pee Preston got up and took it over. When Nagasaki came back he asked Preston, very politely, if he could have his chair back because he wanted to take his boots off. 'Fuck off,' said Preston. Nagasaki reasoned with him gently, for several minutes, just as if we had the vicar in for tea, until Preston told him to fuck off once too often. Nagasaki swooped. He copped Preston's head under his arm in a Grommet, a killingly painful hold, scurfed him across the room and shot him half way up the wall, hanging him from the top of a tallboy with his legs dangling. 'Now stay out of my chair or I'll kill you, you silly little twit,' he said. Then Preston fell off the tallboy, dropped in a heap, and we all burst out laughing.

Not so funny, however, was the dust-up between two good friends, Les Kellett and Clayton Thomas. I was the only one left in the dressing room with them when war broke out. They were head butting, punching, stomping, and doing every sort of evil to each other you could think of. It went on for about fifteen minutes, and I kept shouting: 'Turn it up,' and diving in to pull off one or the other. They took it in turns, throwing me aside, and when it was all over, they were good pals again and I was more battered than either of them.

So much for being a bloody referee.

THREE
COME RASSLING

I can remember a lot of referees and masters of ceremony over the years, but there are only two men in the pro game who transformed these tasks into an art — Lou Marco and George Peake.

Lou Marco, small, thin, with a voice like a worn file, had done very little 'rassling', as he called it. But he knew more about handling a fight than any man alive, and he was as big a draw as many wrestlers. Many millions of television viewers have heard him snapping staccato orders in his rasping voice.

George Peake had presence, authority, a remarkable imagination, and a great capacity for inventing plausible stories off the cuff.

Together, he and Marco were magic. They could get a crowd howling over a fight between two broomsticks, and then arrange a re-match in a week's time which would pack the Albert Hall.

A good referee has to be like Little Red Riding Hood in pantomime. The kiddies scream 'wolf' to warn her what's happening behind her back, but by the time she turns around, the Big Bad Wolf has turned into Granny again, and she looks at the kids as if to say: 'What's all the fuss about?'

Pro punters, not being as polite as kiddies, are likely to call the referee a cretinous blind bastard and offer to buy him a big white stick, and much worse. They don't realise he may know where not to look when villainous fun's afoot, and so they go berserk. When he finally catches on, and wags his finger at one piece of naughtiness, old white-haired ladies at the ringside have apoplexy screaming to tell him that something far more evil is brewing behind his back. Why can't the stupid idiot look where he's supposed to look? Gawd, they could do better themselves. Doesn't he know he can get spectacles, with bloody thick lenses, on the National Health?

Lou Marco was brilliant at stirring, and he'd often do more to drive the crowd into a frenzy than the villains. But at the end of the fight, he'd get a round of applause. He frequently got one from wrestlers, too, for he saved more fighters from getting the bird than any man in the game.

'Cunt,' he'd bark (it was his favourite word), 'what are you doing that for? Throw him on the ropes . . . when he comes off go for his legs . . . ' and so on. Under his sympathetic handling, potential pony bouts became winners, and in the early days, it was his skill, together with that of great performers like Eddie Capelli and Johnny Peters — who had more return bouts than anyone — that helped to mould the success of Dale Martin. Often, Lou was the most important man in the groin, and I still think of him in that way.

Sadly, he was knocked down in Brixton Road, near Dale Martin's building, and badly hurt. He did a bit of M.C.-ing after that, but, unhappily, he was lost to the business. The game owes him a lot. Give him another round of applause.

Lou loved to play the boss man, and he was such a prima donna he should have been a ballerina. He regarded the front seat in the truck or coach as exclusively his, and if some hulking heavyweight pinched it, he'd mutter: 'That's my seat', then grumble and sulk all the way home. We all took the piss out of him something rotten, to try to make him sulk some more, and he would go off his rocker.

He was a notorious fag cadger (not that I can say much because I was a pretty big cadger myself at one time), so we would offer him fags with pinholes in them, and 'accidentally' knock his hat off, and that. One night we'd been at him all the way back from Bristol, and by the time we got to Trafalgar Square, he'd had enough. 'Stop the motor, Pallo,' he barked. 'I'm getting out.' The other lads said: 'Take no notice, Jackie, he can get out when everybody else does'. So I drove on. Lou made his way to the back of the old ambulance, and opened the door. 'All right Pallo, if I kill myself it's down to you.' Tibor Szakacs, who hadn't been over here long then, got all excited and grabbed hold of him, then put his foot on Lou's throat to hold him down. 'Leave if off, Szakacs,' the other lads shouted. 'He's working. Let him jump.' Poor old Lou.

He got homicidal when somebody doctored the special bag in which he carried his dress suit. On the top he'd put two bottles of Bristol Cream sherry which he'd been given, and when he picked up the bag, it flew open and the two bottles popped out and smashed. I fancy I actually saw steam coming out of his nose. That must have been the world's most monumental sulk.

Both George and Lou had healthy thirsts, and they would argue and bicker like hell over whose turn it was to pull out the fags, or buy a round.

In my early days, I recall travelling down to Weymouth to fight after I'd finished teaching boxing at a school in St John's Wood. When I got into the ring, George came over to me and put one arm around my shoulders.

'Ladies and gentlemen,' he said — and his voice quietened them straight away — 'this boy only left the school, where he teaches boxing, at five o'clock this afternoon (really?), and he has driven through thick traffic, all the way down here (oh yeah?) so that he would not be late to entertain you. He didn't even stop to have a bite to eat . . .'

By the time he'd finished you could almost hear a schoolboy choir singing the Hallelujah Chorus, and my own eyes were a little moist. I got a terrific round of applause, and George had built up so much sympathetic heat I hardly needed to wrestle at all.

George could raise steam heat for a mis-match that normally would have been guaranteed to cure insomniacs, and he made more good return bouts than anyone else ever. He could judge the mood of an audience perfectly, and if he felt the atmosphere was right, at the end of a fight, he'd raise his microphone (without consulting anyone) and say something like: 'Ladies and gentlemen, Jackie Pallo has just challenged the Riverside Rhino to a return match, over ten rounds, two weeks from now to the date.' Then he'd lean towards the Rhino's corner and nod and whisper urgently before turning back to say: 'And yes, ladies and gentlemen, the Rhino accepts the challenge and . . . ' more feverish nodding and whispering to both corners, 'each man is putting up a side stake of £500, winner takes all . . . ' and so on. Of course, nobody had said a word to George, and all he'd whispered to them was: 'Leave it to me, leave it to me,' and they'd pretended to prattle back. But you could be sure, in two weeks' time, that there would be a full house for me and Rhino.

The game today is sadly lacking such characters as George Peake and Lou Marco.

Among other good referees in the 50s and 60s were Bobby Palmer, Joe Hill and Max Wall. Tiny Carr was not bad, something of a carbon copy of Lou Marco. Joe d'Orazio, a hard, powerful man, was very competent, but promoters generally preferred referees to be small, because they made the wrestlers look that much bigger.

I never forgot Bobby Palmer telling me that a good wrestling bout should be like a book, with a beginning, middle and a climax. 'Remember,' he said, 'you never turn to the end of the book first and spoil the story.' He was telling me I should carefully build to the climax of a fight.

Joe Hill gave us all a good laugh when we were doing a televised show from Nottingham. One of the lads was spraying himself with deodorant, and as Joe made for the door, he saw me standing with an aerosol can in my hand, and decided to make himself pong nicely for the cameras. 'Let's have some of that,' he said, nicking the can out of my hand. Then he sprayed his bald head with a gold stripe, and walked out of the door. What a chortle. From then on he was Goldenbonce Hill, and I was very careful with the aerosol I used to paint my wrestling boots.

Referees are frequently involved with the action, dishing out 'public warnings', rucking with the fighters, being 'accidentally' knocked out, or deliberately tied up in the ropes and given the treatment. Maybe the referee — a good ex-wrestler — would turn on the geezer who had given him more stick than he could take, and scurf him around the groin. The punters loved that. 'Take both the buggers on yourself, ref.' The rules of the game, which Kent Walton talks about so earnestly ('Now that *is* against the rules. I don't see how the referee can let him get away with that') are invoked only often enough to give the whole affair credibility.

Occasionally, a referee might perform another important service. He produced blood. Real blood. From the wrestlers, that is. With a sliver of razor blade taped to one finger, the merest edge showing, he'd bend over the fighters to check a hold, hand outstretched, and the blade would go in. The doctored fighter would then receive several hefty whacks from his opponent on the spot where the skin was sliced. Blood would then flow. Crowds, as everyone knows, tend to bay for blood. So the lads would spread the available gore around as much as possible, to ensure maximum baying.

Wrestlers also did their own cutting. Once, on television, I had a blade taped to my finger, intending to nick my opponent's ear lobe which — as anyone who's ever cut one shaving knows — bleeds a lot, for ever. The idea is to palm the blade to the referee, for disposal, after you'd used it. This night, without a word of a lie, I forgot all about the blade. But what with clasping hands, interlocking fingers and whatnot, the other wrestler's hands got quite cut up, and when we went back to the dressing room he couldn't understand why he was bleeding like a little porker. He thought he had some sort of obscure disease. I said nowt.

I didn't like using the blade. It made me nervous, and never was this more obvious than when I fought at Belle Vue. I went to snick my man, missed completely, and cut my own shoulder badly instead. There's still a scar there today. I started to bleed, and I worked the blade to the referee. I couldn't believe my mince pies when I saw him casually throw it into the front row of seats. I nodded to my opponent and hissed: 'Throw me out, throw me out'. Over the top rope I went, scattering seats. I was scrabbling around on the floor, trying to find the bloody thing before a punter picked it up, when a bloke bent over me and whispered in my shell-like: 'Can't you find the blade then?' I was bleeding all over the floor, and I never did find it. I reckon that punter had it all the time. The referee, the berk, said he thought it was just a piece of plaster I'd had covering a cut.

Personally, I preferred to bite my own lip to produce blood. I did it many times. However, I knew about the blade trick long before I got into wrestling. Grandfather told me the bare knuckle fighters used it to work up a bit of excitement.

Ah, but if referees may be bent, then who do they call in to referee the championship matches? You may well ask. Surely *they* can't be bent? Well, there is no such animal as a real champion in pro wrestling. The game does not have any Board of Control, like boxing, so no records are kept. No officials, who work strictly to regulations, are appointed at wrestling 'championships', and no appointed doctor sits at the ringside. Have you ever heard of a wrestler fighting a series of eliminators to earn himself a crack at a title? Ever seen a wrestler weigh in? Of course not, because nobody cares a damn how much he weighs. It's all done by size. If he's big, he's a heavyweight. If he's middle-sized he's a middleweight, and so on. What could be simpler?

Perhaps the punters are bored with Smith being World Lightweight Champion, so it can be arranged for Bloggs to win it from him. It may be convenient for Jones to be Commonwealth Lightweight Champion for a week to liven up bouts in the north. You can be champion of Ireland, South Wales, the World, Rutland, Sri Lanka, the Southern Area, the Nor' by Nor' East Area, West Stepney, or any other place you care to think up.

I take it I've made my point. 'Champion' means very little.

In the 50s, championship matches used to draw more because there weren't ninety-five champions around, and wrestling had more standing. The M.C. would announce: 'Ladies and gentlemen, next week we have a championship match and, unfortunately, because of the cost, the price of the seats will be increased by one shilling'. Perhaps the wrestlers would get £3 extra on the night, which wasn't bad for those days.

For quite a long time championship titles were awarded to the shooters who were the best at their weight (or size!), for the sake of appearances, though the fighters chosen didn't necessarily put bottoms on seats. However, a switch could still be worked when a change was needed.

One company manufactured their own championships'

Lonsdale-type belts. Eric Taylor, an excellent wrestler, had one when he left the company, and I'm told that when they asked for it back, Eric said: 'Certainly, as soon as you can find someone who can beat me'. Another great shooter, Brian Maxine, billed as welterweight champ, was known as Gold Belt Maxine. He made the belt himself, and very impressive it was. It all became absurd when wrestlers working for small promoters all over the country started making up belts out of bits of leather, horse brasses, and anything that would shine.

Wrestling isn't like boxing, where fans go to see genuine champions who are also good performers. Wrestling punters go to see performers who are not necessarily the best wrestlers. So I didn't want a title. I was happy with my Mr TV tag. Nobody could take that away from me.

But, eventually, I won the light middleweight title. I was ever so happy when I 'lost' it, at Paisley, two weeks later.

FOUR
NIGGLY AND NUTTY

Not everyone in the game rates Mick McManus as a wrestler. But what a professional, what a lovely worker, what an actor, what a magnificent baddie. Certainly he is one of the best performers the business has ever had, and he became very famous. His fame, however, has a lot to do with me.

Mick got into the game some time before me, but we wrestled each other quite a lot in the early 50s, and he became quite a formidable villain. But his image seemed on the wane when I decided that he and I, with our contrasting styles of villainy, could make a lot of money together.

Mick was fighting at Wembley when I made my move. The show was being televised live, and when I jumped onto the side of the ring, and hung onto the ropes, the cameras swivelled to focus on me. I pointed at Mick. 'I want you, McManus,' I shouted. 'I want you. Fight me if you dare . . .' and so on. He got up and started waving his arms and shouting back, and that's how the greatest series of grudge fights in the history of the game — spanning almost a decade — began. It made both our careers.

At first, Johnny Dale, managing director of Dale Martin, was furious, because it was taboo for one of their wrestlers to pull a stunt without getting clearance from the office. 'You'll never work again,' he told me.

'John,' I said, 'you'll be falling over yourself to book me.'

Mick agreed: 'I think you've cracked it,' he told me. 'That'll pack a few houses.' He was quick to see that we could both make money if we worked on promoting the needle between us.

The public agreed, too. Sackloads of letters arrived at the TV studios, and at Dale Martin's office in Brixton, from punters demanding to see the match. They were full of advice on how I should dismember him and how he should tear off my bollocks. Johnny Dale smiled at me and admitted it was going to be very good for business.

And so it started. At every hall I went to I screamed: 'I want

McManus,' and told the punters exactly what I would do to him. He was equally descriptive about me. In newspaper interviews and television appearances we snatched at every opportunity to express our contempt for each other. When we both appeared on the Eamonn Andrews show we had a blazing row, and he stormed off, refusing to appear on the same set as me. All good publicity.

When Mick started putting his name to a newspaper column, he took every chance he could to slag me off. Lovely stuff. I told him that meals on wheels were making him fat.

Eventually, we became so well known that even craggy old buggers living in remote Highland crofts reacted at the mention of our names. Not very agreeably, perhaps, but villains aren't supposed to be lovable, and when we appeared before the cameras on Cup Final days, eleven million people tuned in to see if the blond, pigtailed, flashy, arrogant, cocksure bastard could beat the scowling, snarling villain who looked like a particularly poisonous Dracula. He was always immaculate, in black shoes, white socks, black trunks. Even what's left of his hair is black, though I'll tell you a secret: if he forgot to dye it, it would soon turn silver.

We had some great matches around the halls, with Mick, the more experienced man, usually getting the verdict, while I was 'unlucky'. In reality, need I say, I know I could have beaten him hopping about on one leg. On television he was billed as 'unbeaten on TV', and I was billed as 'Mr TV'! In fact, our big fights in 1963 and 1965 ended as evil, brutal draws, paving the way for yet a further re-match.

Now this 'unbeaten on TV' bit led to a tale which was the talk of the business for some time afterwards. It was supposed to be the game's equivalent of the Gunpowder Plot, and apparently was sparked off by the animosity which some promoters felt for each other. (I mean, there were those who wouldn't even travel on the same train.)

Anyway, the 'plan' was hatched when Mick was matched against a hard nut and good wrestler from the north, to appear in a televised show at Lime Grove, London. The story relates that Mcmanus should have won by a knockout in the fourth round, but it was whispered in his opponent's ear that it would be a very good thing if he wasn't knocked out. What a sensation it would cause if, instead, he were to pull off two spectacular falls or a knockout against McManus, thus becoming the first man to beat him on the box. Who would be the hero of the punters? After that McManus's conqueror could become a big star. What a good idea. But McManus was not to be hurt as he was due to fight in the north the following week, and they needed him to fill all the seats.

Came the fight and, at the end of round three — so the story goes — Mick muttered: 'O.K. next round I knock you out,' to which the reply was: 'Balls'. After the bell, Mick apparently desperately tried to achieve the knock out but when it became obvious that things weren't going to plan Mick punched his man and followed up by trying to pull down his shorts. The referee had no option but to disqualify Mick and so, though he technically lost, he hadn't *really* in the eyes of the punters. It would appear that quick thinking had won the day for Mick. It was three years before the man concerned fought in London again, and, to my knowledge, he never fought Mick again.

Mick and I were the southern gods of Dale Martin, and there is no doubt our success caused a certain amount of enmity and jealousy in the north, where they wanted one of us dethroned.

In the game, Mick was known as 'Niggly', and his personal nickname for me was 'Nutty'. Heaven knows why. I enjoyed working with him, as the way in which we read each other's moves was almost telepathic. We are both 'light' workers, and never laid hands on each other with undue pressure. Only once was Mick hurt as a result of fighting me. He had just climbed out of the ring, after one of our major bouts, when J.J. (then 10 years old) ran up to him, said: 'You hurt my dad,' and kicked him very hard on the shin. Mick limped to the dressing room and told me: 'Fuck it, I've just done 20 minutes with you without feeling a thing, then your kid nearly kills me outside the ring'.

Nevertheless, J.J. always got along with Mick rather better that I did. For although there was *never* any wrestling needle between Mick and me (the whole thing was an act), we were not mates outside the ring. Neither were we enemies. But there was a little 'feeling'.

With many of his other opponents, Mick refused to give and take. He seemed to insist on destroying them, instead of giving them a good finish, and when he became a matchmaker, in the 60s, I felt that he too often used his influence to his own advantage. Mick seemed to pick the plums, would generally put himself on second — the best spot — and avoided the long trips except when there was big money involved.

He pulled one or two neat tricks on me. At the Albert Hall he mis-matched me with a Frenchman who did a gay act. The first thing this character did after the bell was to kiss me full on the lips. I kissed him back with my fist, and as soon as he left the ring, Jackie Dale sacked him. He left for France the same day. Once, after wrestling Ricki Starr at Leeds, I asked Mick to put him on with me at another Albert Hall promotion, as I thought Ricki a fine performer. But, Mick put himself on with Ricki and landed me with some unknown from Spain at the bottom of the bill.

People still talk to me about my fights with Mick in awed and reverent tones, and sometimes I'm hard put to it not to smile. Thinking back, I realise now that Mick and I hogged the limelight for far too long. We prevented a lot of good youngsters from getting a chance to shine. We were too greedy.

Today Mick collects antiques, and shows the flag, acts as ambassador, and mixes with important people. He's very good at it.

On the rare occasions we meet, he always says: 'No one ever created as much heat as you and me, Nutty'. He's right, of course.

FIVE DEEP HEAT AND WITCHY POO

DEEP HEAT AND WITCHY POO

Heat, or frenzy, agitation, hyper-emotion, call it what you want, can do terrible things to people, and I was very good at producing it. My uncle Tom, who I liked very much, died of a heart attack while watching me and McManus fighting on the screen, and two punters popped off at Bristol and Southampton when their tickers packed up under the strain of over-excitement. Many others have been treated by ambulancemen, or even taken to hospital, as a result of 'heat' sickness.

At the Embassy, in Birmingham, it nearly killed *me*.

I was fighting Vic Faulkner, a blue-eye, and such a clean fighter you could eat your dinner off him. When he went to dropkick me, I stepped aside, and my clenched fist went up, pow, right between his legs. All moody, naturally. I swear I never touched him. But Vic went down, holding himself and writhing about, just as he should, and I waited for him to recover after a bit, as he didn't usually die to my stuff for long. This time was different. He rolled about, face screwed up in agony, moaning like the end of it was caught in a thumbscrew. I was disqualified, and he was helped out, still hamming like mad.

I heard a man shout: 'Let's get the bastard,' and another: 'Let's lynch the fucking swine,' then the crowd went raging crackers. They surged forward, pressed against the ring, and it shook a little and fell off its jacks. I was petrified. The few policemen who were there couldn't do much, and the other wrestlers all came out and fought their way to the ring to help get me out in one piece. Just outside the dressing room the big second with me, *my* second, punched me full in the stomach, glared at me and pushed off. I discovered the silly bugger thought I'd really hurt Vic.

Police reinforcements arrived, and it took them a long time to clear the hall. But the punters didn't go home. They just surrounded the building waiting for me to come out, and they started chanting: 'We want Pallo'. It went on for hours. The ring was dismantled, the seats put away, but outside the message was still the same: 'We're gonna get Pallo. We're gonna get Pallo.' I was not happy, and neither were the police officers who kept nipping in for consultations. In the end, getting on for 1 a.m., we hatched a plot. Tony St Clair, a new young wrestler, and a friend of mine, went outside, got into my car, and drove it through the crowd, right into the hall. I nipped in he nipped out and off I went. The punters erupted and the police heaved back. I drove through with boots and other things banging the roof and sides of my brand new motor. A lot of fun. When I told Vic Faulkner that he'd nearly got me killed, he grinned and said I should be careful where I put my hands.

Some time later, two Irish wrestlers who lived in Brum confessed to me that they'd got their mates in the audience to stir things up something horrible, just for a bit of a laugh. Ho, ho.

Mind you, it wasn't unusual for a wrestler to get amongst the punters and ruck another performer for a chuckle. Sometimes it helped the bout along. It didn't at Brighton Ice Rink, the day that Yuri Borienko, a very tasty Russian — who appeared in a couple of James Bond films — was making heavy weather of it in the groin. 'You dirty Communist git,' I bawled from the crowd. 'Bolshie shithouse.' When I went into the dressing room he clocked my nose so hard it hasn't been the same since. He was far too massive to hit back, so I asked why. 'I thought you mean what you say,' he told me. Idiot!

Now I've chatted to gawd knows how many really nice wrestling punters, but it must be said that I've suffered more damage from punters than I've ever had done to me by another wrestler — apart from the idiot Frenchman who kicked me in the mouth in Paris. I've been trodden on, jumped on, kicked everywhere it can hurt, and had every different size and shape of bottle and can thrown at me. In my early days, all the bottles were glass, and I was concussed several times when they found my nut. We villains were all very thankful when plastic took over and gave us a little relief.

Jackie holds Vic Faulkner in a Pig's Trotter.

ABOVE:
Tag match at Liverpool stadium. Jackie and Alan Dennison at the ropes with Sid Cooper and Alan Colbeck on the floor.

OVERLEAF:
The striped trunks and gold boots became a trade mark.

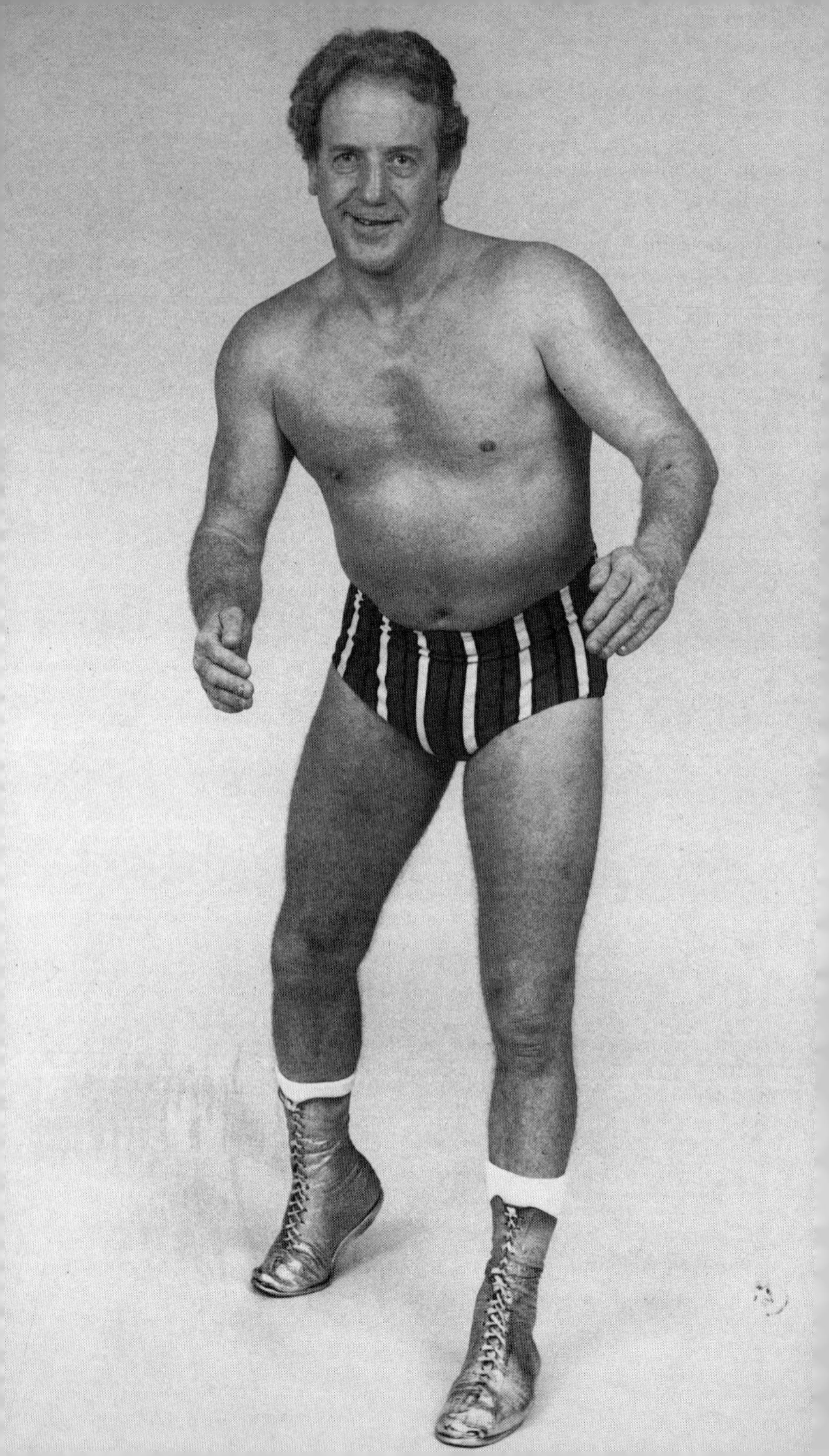

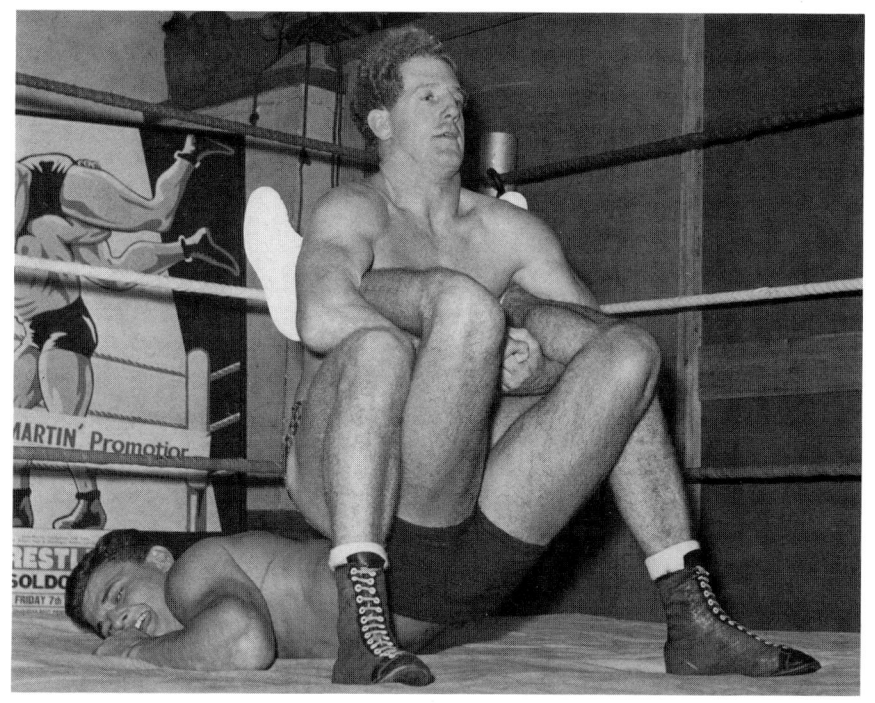

Posed pictures from an Evening News *series on wrestling in the early 60s. Kalmen Gaston is caught in a Boston Crab...*

...and a Flying Drop Kick.

Caricature of Jackie with Mick McManus by Sid Parker.

RIGHT:
Spanish wrestler, Modesto Aledo, gets Head Dropped at Hove Town Hall.

BELOW:
Johnny Eagles in a Head Mare.

DEEP HEAT AND WITCHY POO

I remember rucking with a character sitting beside the ring at Rochester, when suddenly he got up and moved a few feet to the ropes. I couldn't believe it. He must have been sitting in a hole, because there we were, almost eyeball to eyeball. He was about five feet across and had hands like mechanical shovels. 'Get in 'ere, you big slob,' I snarled. As I said, I'm a good actor. Oh dear, what if he had taken me up on it? Again, at Banbury, a huge gypsy jumped into the ring. One of the wrestlers chinned him, but he just came on without pausing for breath. So the other lad hit him and hurt his hand so badly he was hopping about. The first man had another go and broke his finger, while the second forgot his hand long enough to try a dropkick, which the gypsy barely noticed. Our heroes were about to leave the ring to him, when a posse arrived from out back, and old Romany was dragged out with men waving about on the ends of his arms. Some men are very hard.

At Doncaster I nearly got nicked for hitting someone. I'd gone out of the ring, and while I was on the floor this fellow stood up and kicked me, very painfully, in the ribs. I got up and went to give him a good slap across the face, with my open hand, just to show him I wasn't amused. He threw his head back, and I hit his girlfriend in the boat race instead. Murder! The police suggested I should try an apology. I did, she accepted, and was decent enough to admit it all happened because her boyfriend kicked me.

Women could be poisonous. They tend to believe everything about the game is genuine, and get steamed up more quickly than men. Timid housewives and elderly ladies with mauve rinses are usually the worst. The things they scream! If they'd had their way with three bits of my anatomy, I'd have been able to get a job in a Turkish harem years ago. They are very nifty with hatpins. The number I've had stuck in my backside, some up to the hilt, I couldn't guess at. Once I went back to the dressing room with one still embedded in one of my cheeks. I've seen ladies puffing at cigarettes to get a good glow at the end, so that they could stub them out on me if I got within range. Sometimes they succeeded.

At other times they'd grab my legs while I was standing up

against the ropes, so I couldn't move without falling over. Then I'd get the pins and needles treatment.

But worst of all were the handbags. The blue rinse brigade would come with a giant-sized jar of cold cream stuck in one corner of their handbags. Get hit on the nut with one of those, and you know all about it. One woman threw her handbag at me. I quickly swooped down, shovelled in all the bits and pieces and handed it back to her, with a bow. Afterwards her husband came around, and said he thought I was a real gent and that he'd like to buy me a drink. But did she come around? Oh no.

I've had sharpened pencils stuck in my ears, and my head's been dented uncountable times by the stiletto heels of dainty little shoes. Go over the ropes and land amongst a bunch of angry female punters, and, believe me, you're glad to get back into the civilised safety of the groin.

When I was fighting Pat Selvo at Bermondsey Baths a fellow in the second row called me a cunt. He was sitting next to a really gorgeous bit of crumpet, so I leaned over the ropes and said: 'Sir, do you realise there's a young lady sitting next to you?' expecting a grateful smile from the lovely dolly. Instead, she opened her north and south and bawled, in a voice that would crack a pint glass: 'Oh bollocks, get on with it!' I believe it was the same night that a charming old lady came up to me in the street, and said how much she admired me and would like to shake hands with me. I obliged, and she still had hold of my right when she swung her left. I was only a shade too quick for her. I tell you, they're dangerous at any age.

Mind you, a lot of it was my own fault. I felt that the punters weren't getting their money's worth unless I manipulated them into really hating me, and promoters sometimes ticked me off for working up mass hysteria.

I had a gimmick finish that really stirred them up. If the referee disallowed my fall, I'd do a big thing. The stupid bugger was obviously against me, wasn't he, and I'd go into a sulk and walk out of the ring in disgust, refusing to come back.

Banter, repartee and rucking were also an important part of the act, and sometimes the chat could be very amusing. We were last on the bill when I wrestled Eddie Capelli at Norwich Cattle Market Hall one night, and that's the worst spot because the punters are getting restless, ready for a last pint, or supper and a good kip. Somebody shouted in a bored voice: 'Pallo, I'm leaving you the keys. Put out the lights when you go, all right?' Someone else said: 'Don't you touch the lights, I'm checking me pools,' and a third man chimed in with: 'Go on? You tried that new perm in the *Mirror*?' Sometimes they kept it going for a whole round.

A woman would scream: 'Pallo, you're too bloody big headed'. I'd shout back: 'Darling, if I put my head in your mouth it would rattle about'.

I'd usually pick on two people, one on each side of the ring, and do my best to get the other punters laughing at them. Women were easier to get at it. If I saw a bird eating chocolates I'd jump out of the ring, take the box, eat one, then offer the box to the person next to her. 'Would you like one? Yes. Pass it on. Mustn't be greedy.'

If a man was obviously well dressed, I'd point and say: 'Up early tomorrow, mate. Moss Bros. opens at eight', and I'd get the birds going with retorts like:

'Go and live in India, darling. You'll be sacred over there.'

'I'm doing panto again this year, darling, and we're still short of ugly sisters.'

'Give up that grapefruit diet, darling. It's not working.'

'I've got a castle in Wales, darling. How much would you charge to come and haunt it?'

You could get the men going by niggling them about the money they earned.

'Pallo, you're getting old.'

'Yes, but I'm getting old rich, and you're getting old poor.'

'You're rubbish Pallo.'

'Yes, but your money goes into *my* bank tomorrow.'

'You're not worth a light, Pallo.'

'Wrong.' I'd point at the door. 'We both came in through that, but you paid and I *got* paid. Who's the berk?'

Most crowds lap up this sort of banter, and I'd get the hall in a right buzz. Nevertheless, it was banter which led me to what was probably the worst moment in my career.

I was wrestling at Beckenham Baths, and there was a woman in the audience wearing sunglasses. What an opportunity to take the micky.

'Come on darling,' I said, 'let's get the specs off. The sun's gone in.' Then: 'When you've been around as long as I have, me old luv, you'll realise the sun can't shine through a bleedin' roof'. On and on I went, making a right meal of it, and I thought no more about it until I was told there was a man urgently asking to see me, after the show. It was the husband of the woman in sunglasses, and he wanted me to talk to his wife and tell her I was sorry. Sorry? Why? I asked.

'Well, you see, she's blind,' he said, 'but she doesn't like to advertise it. She got a bit upset at you making such a lot of fun at her expense because she's a very great fan of yours. I always bring her to the wrestling and tell her what's going on.'

I had a hard time keeping the tears back when he introduced me to this lady, and I told her how sorry I was for being such a blind fool myself. She said it was all right, and that I shouldn't upset myself, because I wasn't to know. It was just that things had got on top of her a bit. 'One of the things I like about you is your cheeky sense of humour,' she said. 'I hope to hear a lot more of it.' I gave her a hug and a kiss on the cheek. A brave lady. I hope she's well.

A funny thing about wrestling punters is that they'll accept the hamming, but not the lamming. They are conditioned to exaggeration. In other words, if a fighter grabs his knee and rolls about, beating hell out of the ring in phoney agony, then they'll likely believe he's hurt, and he may even get some sympathy. But when you *really* hurt yourself, it rarely looks good, because you certainly don't feel like doing an act about it. So the punters won't believe it. 'Phoney', 'fake', 'rigged', 'load of rubbish', they shout as you are carted away, gritting your choppers.

It happened like that, for instance, when J.J. broke his collarbone.

DEEP HEAT AND WITCHY POO

In Scotland, of course, they don't care what you break, and if you are anything but Scottish — especially English — the punters prefer to break it for you. Even their geriatrics are a menace. At Paisley I was being shepherded to the dressing room by two policemen after fighting Andy Robbins, when a dear old chap of at least 82 stepped forward, smiling, and cracked me so hard on the chin I nearly fell over. The Old Bill thought this a hoot, and said it was a good job I hadn't bumped into the bloke when he was twenty-one.

Nobody would watch wrestling in Scotland if there weren't Scots on the bill capable of eating wrestlers from other ethnic groups. When J.J. and I wrestled tag at an agricultural show-cum-fête at Perth, they gave us a caravan for our changing room. After the bout, during which we bruised a few egos, we were dressing when all of a sudden there was a noise like the Vikings had landed and several hundred people were outside demanding our blood. The caravan began to shake, and me and J.J. were bouncing around inside, hanging on to anything we could. The caravan was on the verge of teetering over when the bobbies arrived in force and a grand battle started outside. That was a bit iffy, particularly as J.J. and me had been told they were 'friendly' in Perth.

We reckoned the mob must have come up for the day from Glasgow and Edinburgh, as these are the places to wrestle if you want to know what the Christians felt like when the Romans let out the lions.

At Glasgow, punters believe that God lives at the Kelvin Sports Arena and speaks like Will Fyffe. At the Eldorado Stadium, in Edinburgh, everybody knows that Robbie Burns is king and that they live in the capital of Britain. In these places, the groin is the wrestler's haven of rest. The walk from the ring to the dressing room is no man's land.

Except, that is, for the night I fought the great Scot, George Kidd, at Glasgow. I'd just done something nasty to George when the referee shouted: 'Quick, Jackie. Get out!' I looked around, and there was this large lad climbing through the ropes, waving a huge bayonet, looking at me with bloodshot eyes as if I was the dish of the day. Probably kebab. Talk about

'Beam me up, Scottie'. I disappeared in a blink, and stayed in the dressing room, not a little nervous, until the police had got rid of the maniac.

At Edinburgh, they employ a small army of stewards to stop you getting killed by the punters, and they surround you when you leave the ring to walk down a long corridor. On both sides, the punters are snarling like madmen, punching, gouging, kicking and throwing things, and the corridor isn't wide enough to escape them. If you veered from the right, they'd get you on the left, and the other way around. Naturally, I had to carry on keeping up my image, sneering in contempt, cocksure and arrogant. I wouldn't kowtow to the bums, even if I was scared silly.

I could put up with all this. But there was one thing they did in both cities that the punters never did anywhere else. They spat at you. Even the women. It made J.J. and me feel very murderous.

The trick is to walk slowly when you leave the groin. That way it is difficult for them to trip you. Up there they like to play 'kick the wrestler when he's down'.

No, I don't dislike Scotland, or the Scots. I have met — and continue to meet — very many excellent Scottish folk. I'm simply saying that their wrestling fans are mainly graduates from Bedlam.

Which brings me back to women. They would certainly have made bedlam of my marriage if I let them. Especially Witchy Poo. That was the nickname she was christened with. Who knows why? It just fitted. And Witchy Poo pursued me for 12 years, all over the country. Even if I walked into the ring in Carlisle, there she'd be. Oh my gawd! I'm bloody sure the other lads used to tell her where I was on next, because that's the way the bastards are. They'd see her at the ringside and say: 'Jesus, but I'd love to give you one,' and Witchy Poo would recoil and answer: 'Oh no, I'm saving myself for Jackie'. When I was wrestling, she'd run up to the ring and scream: 'I love you, I love you, I love you . . .' like the needle had got stuck in the record.

I kept telling Witchy Poo that she should find herself

another fellow, as I really loved my wife, Trixie, who travelled with me to most of the shows anyway, thank goodness, and could see that W.P. wouldn't have much chance of making the centre spread of *Playboy*.

But the more I ignored Witchy, the more she persisted, and she even rang up Trixie to tell her she was sorry, but she loved me to distraction, and couldn't help herself. She also collared J.J. and told him how much she wanted to be his mother and, indeed, would have been if things had worked out differently. I could never sort out her reasoning on that one. Witchy Poo had a funny, nasal voice, very similar to that of Kenneth Williams, particularly when she said: 'Hullo'. I didn't see her for some time, and then, one night she came up to me and J.J. with a bloke on her arm, after a show. 'Hullo,' she said shyly. 'I'd like you to meet my husband.' He put out his hand and said 'Hullo' in *exactly* the same voice as hers. We had Kenneth Williams times two, as if one wasn't enough. J.J. and me looked at each other, and we nearly split our spleens trying not to laugh as we wished them well. All the best, Witchy Poo. You didn't do anyone any harm.

I was having a beer in the bar at Wimbledon one night, after a show, when this bloke comes up, introduces an Olympic standard bird as his wife, and starts chatting. The wife is twinkling at me, and hubby says she's a tremendous fan of mine, and it would be a real favour if I came home with them and gave her a seeing to. I asked him to say again, and he said: 'The wife would like you to fuck her'. I steadied my stool and asked him how he would be spending the time. 'Me? I like to watch,' he said. I told them to bugger off sharpish.

Again, I booked a first-class sleeper on the train back from Scotland, and I was just settling in when the adjoining door to the sleeper next door rattled, and in walked this nice brunette with a husky brown voice. She was wearing very little, and what there was of it you could see through. As it was in the early hours, I sussed that she had not come to talk about my Japanese Strangle Hold, but I practically had to put it on her to get her out.

Because of such incidents, I always used to lock my door

when staying in hotels, so I was more than surprised to hear a tap on the window while I was dressing in one hostelry. Outside, clinging to the drainpipe, was the woman who owned the place, and I helped her in only because she looked as if she was about to fall off. It turned out that she was very good at hanging on to anything, and it took me some minutes to disentangle myself, collect my gear, and find another empty bedroom.

One night, I went out of the ring, and landed almost in the lap of a nice young bird. 'Sorry about that, love,' I said. 'Meet me in the bar afterwards,' she said, 'and you can spend the rest of the night on my lap.' Cheeky.

We'd wrestled at the Ice Rink, in Ayr, one evening, and I was sharing an hotel room with a wrestler who's a good pal of J.J. and me. In the groin he does a poof act. Outside it, he concentrates on birds. Anyway, he went out, and I turned in about 11.30 p.m. I was half asleep, when I became aware of a girl, who couldn't have been more than 17, undressing in the gloom by the bed. She was about to get in with me when zoom, out I got the other side. I picked up her panties, bra, dress and coat, hustled her to the door, and left her naked, in the corridor, with her clothes around her feet, looking very bewildered.

About three o'clock, I woke up to find my room mate shaking me, somewhat steamed up. 'You conceited bastard,' he said, 'that bird was for me, not you.' How should I know? She wasn't wearing a label. Then he explained. He'd dated two girls. After pulling the first, he'd arranged to meet the second in the hotel room, and given her the key. When I chucked her out, she'd walked down the road and bumped into him kissing girl number one goodnight in a shop doorway. The two girls were not very pleased, and neither was the great lover, as he hadn't got very far with the first.

One Eastern European wrestler also fancied himself as a great lady-killer. He was always boasting, in fractured English, about the latest young woman who had gratefully surrendered her virginity to him, but all the females we saw him with were pushing pensionable age. We were drinking in

Tommy Mann's club in Manchester one night — Tommy later did a lot of film stunt work — and loverboy was smiling and buggering up his vowels, telling us of his new conquest, when we were joined by a rather attractive brass. She turned to him and said: 'Come off it luv, you're just a little rabbit,' which, in prostitute talk meant someone who gets about one out of ten for lovemaking. 'I never touch her, I never touch her,' he said becoming more difficult to understand as he got excited. But we told him to give it a rest, because when a brass says something like that, she really means it. For ages we drove him mad calling him Rabbit, or Bunny. Gawd knows how many fresh lettuces the lads bought him.

Wrestlers have their own code about females. For instance, it is strictly taboo to take out a girl who is under 16, even if she looks — and claims to be — a lot older. The lads reckon it's up to a bloke to make sure, and if *anybody* breaks the rule, he gets a very heavy sorting out from the others, sometimes for several weeks. Wrestlers really loathe men who attack children, rape young girls, and beat, mug and rape the old and defenceless. There would be a sharp decrease in this kind of crime if wrestlers were left to deal with those found guilty of it.

Also, with few exceptions, wrestlers are faithful to their wives. Certainly much more so than husbands in any other branch of showbusiness. Especially me. If I made a pass at another bird, the lads would probably club together and send me to see a trick cyclist, as I'm the bloke many of them asked to look after their wives, or girl friends, while they were taking a shower. Incidentally, trying to pull someone else's wife, or steady girl, is another offence which is likely to land you with broken bones.

As I said, my Trixie came to many shows with me (I once delighted the crowd by nipping out of the ring to kiss her, to celebrate a fall), and one night, at Chelmsford, this French wrestler, Jean Murrant, told me how he'd been chatting up this lovely girl. When he pointed her out, I said to leave it off as it was the wife. 'Sorree Jackee.' Next night we're fighting at Watford, and while I'm in the ring I see him chatting up Trixie again. So thinking he may not know about our code, and might find it painful, I told George Peake, the M.C. to have a quiet word with him, which he did.

Murrant was so soree he almost cried.

'But you tried the same thing last night, too,' I said. Old Jean looked astonished.

'But she wear a different 'at,' he said. 'Ow can I tell?'

J.J. always says to me: 'Dad, I admire your morals, but don't expect me to live up to them'. Which is fair enough as he's a bachelor, and the bachelor boys in the game don't have to hunt around for women. The Ring Rats — wrestling's equivalent to the pop world's groupies — go after them.

There are many fewer Ring Rats around these days because not enough good looking youngsters, with beautiful bodies, are coming into the business. In the 60s, hundreds of girls used to shriek at the violence and drool over rippling muscles and bulging trunks. Some towns, particularly Southampton and Torquay, were notorious for the girls. At Southampton the pier was done out with palm trees and lots of little alcoves. What went on in the alcoves was very hot indeed. It's a wonder the palm trees didn't wilt.

Hundreds of Scandinavian students used to come over to Torquay, and they flocked to the wrestling. Some of them were really beautiful. I reckon they used to fantasise that the boys were fighting over them. But enough of that, I've done the psychiatry bit already. Anyway, there were two dressing rooms both sides of the stage at Torquay, joined by a dark corridor under it, and if you were in a hurry to get from one dressing room to another, you had to have a side-step like a rugby fly half to avoid tripping over the undulating bodies. Sorry mam, sorry mam, sorry Sam. It's a wonder some of them didn't suffer permanent damage.

It was not unusual to come out and find a girl, or two, draped across the bonnet of your car, waiting for a bit of nooky, and when we used the coach, or whatever, we many, many times got fed up with waiting for lads who were with birds, and drove off to let them find their own way home.

Seventy-five per cent of wrestlers have excellent physiques, but I never had a great-looking body, except in comparison to the average man. However, this didn't seem to put the birds off. They used to give me the come on something terrible — more so when I was over fifty, funnily enough — and I was always getting cigarette packets and pieces of paper pushed into my hand, with addresses and telephone numbers on them, or instructions to meet a bird at a certain place at a certain time. And many times I've been groped by women when I was out and about, shopping and that, sometimes even when Trixie was with me. Well-heeled, well-preserved middle-aged ladies were the worst. I was in Harrods with Trixie once when I felt a hand come between my legs from behind, and I was grabbed. You know where. I looked around, and there was this really elegant, stunning woman of about forty, grinning at me, full of mischief. 'Not today, thank you,' I said.

And the letters, thousands of them. Talk about descriptive writing. Women can be far more dirty-minded than men. Not that I didn't get letters from men too. Homosexuals seemed to get very excited over the velvet ribbon I wore on my pigtail, and they'd send me bits of ribbon and ask me to tie it around you know where before sending it back. Nutty kooks.

I never kidded myself that it was my devastating charm and good looks that pulled the birds. I believe they considered me a challenge, a nut they wanted to crack, because I ignored all their come-ons and open invitations. Not that I haven't been tempted. I'm no monk.

It's just that I dearly love my Trixie and would never do anything to hurt her. We go back a long way together.

SIX THWACKS, GRUNTS, GROANS AND GUTTERIDGE

I'm a much better boxer than I am a wrestler, and before everybody falls about and says, oh yes, doesn't it bloody well show, let me explain that I was born into a boxing family.

My real name is Gutteridge, and for many years my cousin, Reg, was boxing correspondent of the London *Evening News*. He still ranks amongst the best commentators and writers on the sport.

I nicked the name Pallo from my brother-in-law, Frank, who's an executive with Kodak in America. He didn't seem to mind, and it pacified the rest of the family, who weren't exactly in stitches at the thought of the Gutteridge name — respected in pugilism — being dragged around a wrestling groin. In any case, I thought Jackie Pallo fitted the bill better than Jackie Gutteridge. After all, how far would Archie Leach have got if he hadn't changed his name to Cary Grant? The comparison is obvious.

I was born above the gymnasium my father owned in Britannia Road, Islington, London, and probably the first sounds I heard were the thwacks of leather on flesh, the grunts of wrestlers, and the groans of weightlifters.

When I got a bit bigger my grandad, Arthur Gutteridge, would carry me downstairs to watch his son Jack, my dad, helped by his twin brother, my Uncle Dick, working with the bevy of boxers who used the gym. British Lightweight Champion Bill Thompson, and Middleweight Champion Albert Finch were among those they later trained, so they didn't do so badly. Indeed, Dad also sparred with Primo Carnera, and helped to train him at St Bride's Institute, just off Fleet Street, London, when he was on his way to becoming World Heavyweight Champion. Primo took to wrestling when his boxing days were over, and we both wrestled on the same bill at Brighton. Afterwards, when we talked about the old days and my old man, the big chap rubbed his chin, smiled, and said: 'I remember best his left hook'.

Grandad was a toff, a real gent, and a lovely character. For many years he trained and seconded at the National Sporting Club, in London, and he became knucklefight Lightweight Champion of England. Family lore has it that he was the first of the professional barefist fighters to lace on the new-fangled boxing gloves, at the club in 1888, but he told me he never liked them as much as his own knuckles. Naturally, Grandad taught his sons to box.

My Dad went off to fight in the Great War and became Army Lightweight Champion. Then he was blinded for five months as a result of one of the first mustard gas attacks the Germans made in France. When he came home he wanted to turn professional boxer, but Grandad, whose word was law, said no, he didn't want to see his lad blinded for life, and that was that.

In those days, Grandad's high-class mates at the Sporting Club sometimes asked him to accompany them to fights, as they valued his opinion on the young prospects they fancied. One day he was asked, by Lord something or other, to go with him to The Ring, the famous boxing hall at Blackfriars, to run his eye over a boy called Bob Wilson, who his lordship considered very good. This Grandad did, and he was not at all happy to discover that Bob Wilson was, in reality, his son Jack, who'd been determined to carry on boxing without his father finding out. Grandad collared him as he climbed out of the ring, and sternly demanded that he solemnly promise, there and then, that he would never again fight professionally. My father, who had won the fight, saw the hurt and concern in his dad's eyes, so he agreed. They shook hands, and from that moment Dad became a trainer. It is said that his lordship dined out on the story for several weeks.

So when it came my turn to learn fisticuffs, at the age of seven, there was no shortage of teachers. The first thing my father taught me was never to lose my temper, and I rarely have, throughout my life. I've pretended to, certainly, but that's all part of showbiz. He also explained that a man never loses the power punch, once he has learned to do it properly. Indeed, I sparred with Grandad when he was over eighty. Naturally, the timing was rusty, but couldn't he still whack!

Ideally, said Dad, all fighting should be done inside a ring, but there would come times in life when I would be pushed too far and forced to fight outside one. Then I should go in strong and keep punching until I was on top. This I tried to do. I didn't pick fights, and when I really hurt another boy (smile, you bastards, if you will) I didn't like doing it at all. I thought it was a bit off when they hurt me, too.

Anyway, after all the talking, Dad and I put on the gloves and got into the ring. We faced each other, and then he hit me. Just a tap, but it knocked me back a few feet. 'Always be on guard,' said Dad. 'Always watch out for the other fellow.' Dad coached by example. He'd show me once, show me twice, then show me ouch. He reasoned that two chances were one more than most people would give me, and if I hadn't caught on by then, I needed a painful reminder. After that my memory usually improved, but when I was ten I got a bit too sloppy, and he accidentally knocked me out. Inside the ropes I got a lot of stick from dad, but outside them he never laid a finger on me. We enjoyed mutual respect.

Dad used more or less the same methods when teaching boxing to the boys of Arnold House School, St John's Wood, an excellent preparatory school for the sons of those not short of a bob or two. He took the job in 1924, the year before I was born, and I took over from him when he became ill, 24 years later, carrying on the Gutteridge tradition at Arnold House for a further 25 years. I only gave up the job, in 1973, because it conflicted with my yearly appearances as a nasty in pantomime.

By then I was relishing my passion for the stage proper. I'd always wanted to be a real trouper, but I only found the confidence to try when I became a wrestling star. This was because I've always been slow at reading and writing, despite the brave efforts of the teachers at Queen's Head School, Islington, and I was afraid that I wouldn't be able to learn my lines in time.

My mother, Annie, who's ninety while I'm writing this, says that my obsession to perform in front of others (she calls it 'blooming show-off') first showed itself when I was about six.

It seems that, when visitors called, nobody could stop me from climbing onto the table and screeching out a selection of songs which I called 'opera'. While Mum gnashed her teeth, and anything else gnashable, the visitors smiled in bewildered fashion, quickly made their excuses and left. Mum said she didn't much mind this with people she didn't particularly like, but that it also stopped her mates from popping in for a chat.

I've never lost this ability to empty houses with my voice. Even coaching from the lovely singer, Eve Boswell, had little effect, and the couple of records I made wouldn't have got a mention in the charts of the China Sea. But unfortunately, this doesn't matter in pantomime, because I always play the villain, and when I sing I'm supposed to frighten the children anyway.

Mind you, it didn't quite work out that way in 1971, when I was Bad Baron Heinke in *Goldilocks* at Torquay. Came the moment when I was to sing on stage for the first time ever, and I faced the packed rows of parents and kiddies and snarled: 'All right, all right, now you've all made me very angry, and when I'm angry, grrrr! Now I'm going to scare you, now I'm going to frighten you out of your wits.'

Suddenly, up the centre aisle towards me, tripped a little blonde moppet. She grabbed hold of the band rail, pulled herself up, and piped: 'Go on then, mister, frighten me'. She gazed at me expectantly, and my music started. I opened my mouth and a mumble escaped. I tried again, and the mumble became a croak. Paralysed, I looked to sidestage for help and saw Lionel Blair, the man in charge, hopping up and down frantically beckoning me to come off. Thankfully, I went.

'You'll be all right, don't worry. You'll be all right,' Lionel kept repeating. 'On you go.'

He was dead right. I wasn't going to submit to any three stone female fleaweight. But I must admit that when I walked on I was much relieved to see that somebody had collared the tot and, hopefully, chained her to her seat. I got a loud round of sympathetic applause. It was the only time I ever got applause before singing. Word must have got around.

An early performance — aged 6 — in the school play.

The new boy shows his strength, aged 25.

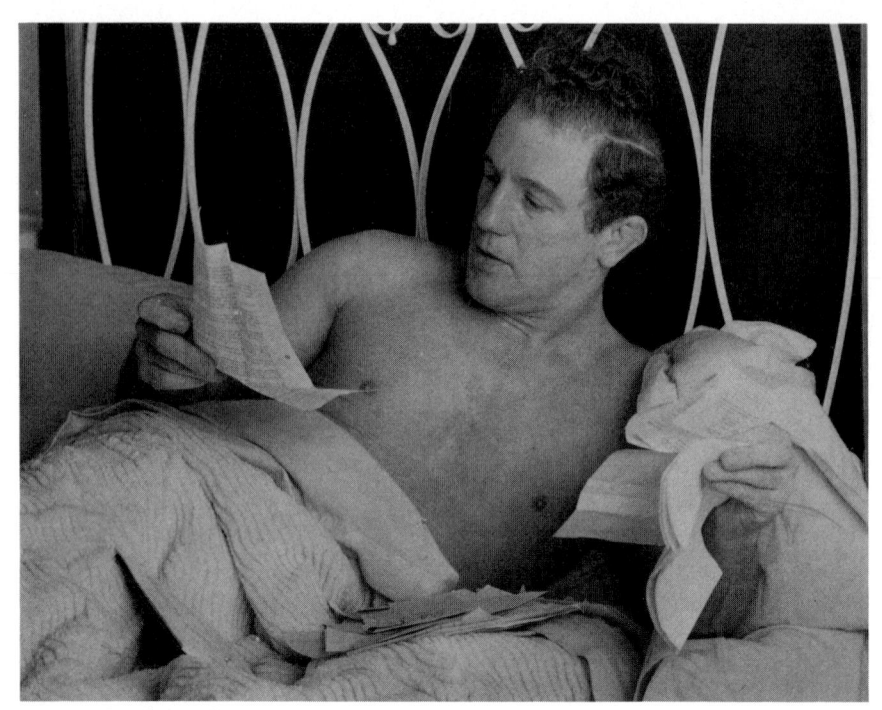

Letters by the sack.

Grooming the famous pigtail.

OPPOSITE:
A specially-made gold lamé suit worn, appropriately, at the Eldorado Stadium, Edinburgh.

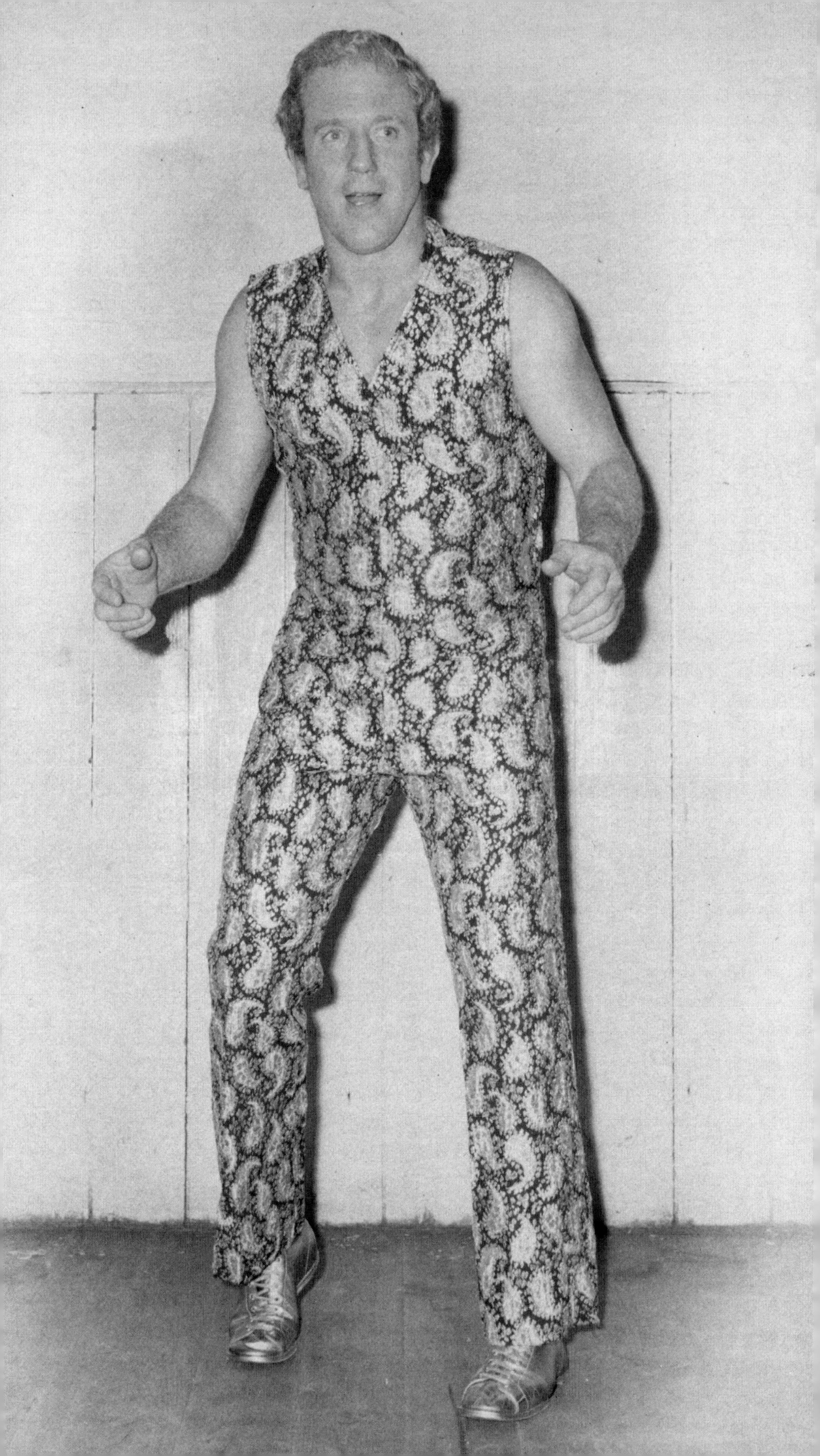

Jackie and Johnny Kwango entertain the Duke of Edinburgh at the Royal Albert Hall, London.

My only stage appearance as a lad was when I took part in a couple of sketches in a Gang Show at Islington Town Hall, which were performed by the 37th North London Scout Troop, of which cousin Reg and I were members for quite a few years.

I learned a little wrestling from my patrol leader, Don Irvin, who competed in the 1958 Olympics, and his brother, Ken, also a fine amateur wrestler, and picked up a few tips watching the wrestlers for whom Dad and Uncle Dick had started to act as seconds, often going with them to bouts at places like Lane's Club, in Baker Street, London. I picked up a few pence doing odd jobs for boxers and wrestlers, and earned a few bob as a numbers boy at wrestling contests. This meant I walked around showing a board which told the punters which round was coming up, just in case they couldn't count.

Once, we were with a bunch of wrestlers going to Hastings for a show, when the coach hit a rabbit which dashed out of the hedge, and Uncle Dick shouted for the driver to stop. The brakes screeched, but Uncle Dick couldn't wait, jumped out while we were still moving, and went arse over tip. The rabbit got away, but Uncle Dick didn't. We had to take him to hospital so they could stitch up the big split in his head. 'Pity,' he said. 'I do fancy a nice fresh rabbit.'

In the mid-30s, wrestling already had a good following, and a good pro often wrestled twice a day, travelling to Birmingham for a morning contest, then fighting at night at one of the South London music halls. It must have been around then that I got the message that there were a few quid to be made. But boxing was Dad's real passion, and so it was with me.

I was a handy scrapper, and didn't get beaten often as a schoolboy. Then I graduated to London Federation boxing and fought my way to the final. On the night of the big fight I had flu, but it made little difference. I met an excellent kid called Clark who gave me a right walloping. I often wondered why he didn't turn pro.

When war was declared, I was fourteen, and when I left

school, shortly afterwards, Dad got me a job as a butcher's apprentice with a friend of his, George Boundy, in Essex Road, Islington. For ten bob a week I started at seven, then worked like a slave until seven at night, except on Saturdays, when it was usually ten before I finished scrubbing and sluicing down every bloody thing (literally) in sight. Butchery and I did not mix, and the thought of spending the rest of my life trying not to cut off my cold fingers with an outsize machete, was not cheering. Still, it was a job, and I stayed on for two years, trimming tiny pieces of meat, cutting out ration coupons, and chipping my fingers, until I finally convinced the foreman at the local munitions factory that I was old enough to do my bit for the war effort. Happily, I said goodbye to Mr Boundy, the offal and the brisket, and two days later I turned up at the factory gates, at 7 a.m., to learn how to become a welder.

I've always liked working with my hands, and it wasn't long before I became pretty good. Everything went well for a long time, until one day, crossing the factory floor, I stooped to peer into the innards of one of the machines to see how it worked (something I often did) — and it scalped me.

I was carted off, bald, bleeding, in pain, not a pretty sight, and off work. But everything began growing again, and in no time I was just as good looking as ever. I thought the top of my head was just like everyone else's, but when it came my turn for call up, the army quacks didn't see it that way and decided they could win without me. Perhaps they thought I was going to butt the Germans.

Meanwhile cousin Reg and I had joined Canonbury Towers Youth Club, and one evening in 1943 I met a new member called Trixie, who was very pretty, slim, blonde and shapely, and who agreed to let me walk her home. We went into an air raid shelter for a goodnight kiss and I tried to make love to her. But Trixie wasn't about to give the all clear, and knew much more about escaping from holds than I did. I was surprised when she said she would meet me again, and flabbergasted when she agreed to marry me, just three weeks later. I was an engaged man; I had to better myself.

I'd always wanted to be a mechanic, so I got a job at Crouch Hill Motors and started my apprenticeship. No problem. I loved the work and hardly noticed a couple of years going by.

Trixie and I were still courting.

I moved on to Godfrey's, the motor cycle specialists in Euston road, where Thames Television Studios now stand, and more years passed with me happily up to my elbows in grease.

Trixie and I continued walking out.

When I moved to Blackman's, in Kentish Town, another motor bike outfit, I was a fully fledged fitter, and I'd probably still be tinkering with engines in somebody's garage today if they'd paid me enough money. But when 1949 arrived I was getting £8 a week, and though that was pretty good pay at the time, I wanted to give Trixie everything.

Trixie and I were still engaged.

By now I knew quite a lot about wrestling. It's a tough sport to learn, but I had a great teacher in George Mackenzie, who'd taught the army boys unarmed combat, and also coached the lads at Ashdown Wrestling Club and at Canonbury Towers. George was a real gent, a big name in the sport, and a one hundred per cent amateur. I was a keen pupil, and he'd brought me to the stage where I was wrestling the occasional bout for real.

Unfortunately it was all for fun, and I kept hearing these tasty tales of pro wrestlers fighting seven days a week and earning £30 odd. This was big money, and I'd already been engaged to Trixie for six years. I couldn't expect her to go for the record. I decided to turn pro.

George Mackenzie was very upset when I told him. He'd considered me a kindred spirit, a good prospect, and here I was, selling out for money. And, as I've said, the family weren't overjoyed either.

But I'd made up my mind, and I went to Brixton to ask Jack Dale and his partner, Les Martin, if they'd take me on. Jackie Dale, a hard fighter, was known in the business as 'Elbows', because he was a bit heavy with them. I wrestled him several times in the gym, and he always gave me a good hiding though he was 20 years older than me. Anyway, he called in Pat Cloak, a good pro, and told me to get in the ring with him and show what I could do.

For ten minutes Pat showed me what I couldn't do. He scurfed and screwed me all over the place. Now when you scurf a man, you rough him up a bit — drag him backwards so he wears his face out on the mat, and things like that. If you screw him, it means that when you get him in a hold you give him a lot of pain. So there I was, in pain, with Jackie Dale telling me I was coming along quite nicely but that I should give it a couple more years. I wasn't good enough yet. Meanwhile, if I wanted to do some seconding, travel to the shows, use the gym, pick up tips from the other pros, then I was welcome. And that was how I began working 17-hour days.

Up early, I'd jump on my bike at our house in Liverpool Road and pedal off to St John's Wood, to take my boxing classes, then race back for a change and nosh and off to the wrestling.

Of course, I knew a lot of the faces, like Black Butcher Johnson, for instance, one of the first black wrestlers, who I met with my father when a very small boy. He was Johnny Kwango's big brother. Then there was Chopper Howlett, Chopper Simms, Bert Mansfield, Tony Mancelli, and great wrestlers like Dave Armstrong and Ernie Baldwin. Most of the old boys had started off as amateurs, and they really knew how to look after themselves. They were bloody hard nuts.

I nicknamed one of the lads Banger Johnson, because he reckoned that if he had to fight long distance, like in Scotland, it was cheaper to buy an old banger for a couple of quid and drive up, than to pay the train fare. When he got back, *if* he got back, he could either flog the car, give it away, or abandon it. Gawd knows how many streets he littered with wrecks.

So there I was, night after night, at St Leonard's, Hastings, Rochester, Peterborough, or wherever, with my bucket and sponge. Unlike in boxing, wrestling seconds don't have to know anything about anything. They simply walk with their man to the ring, wield the sponge or flannel and suchlike, and try to look knowledgeable. But for me the corner of the ring was a good place from which to watch and learn the techniques of pro wrestling, the various holds and moves which different men specialised in, and the art of showmanship in which some were supreme. I also made a point of learning what not to do — the mistakes which displeased and bored the punters.

Among the heavyweight stars then, Bert Asseratti was a big draw, but the man who could always fill a hall was Dirty Jack Pye. He became a pro in the pre-war days when wrestlers tended to give each other cauliflower ears and bent noses, throw bottles and hit each other with buckets, bowls, stools and anything else they could lay their hands on. They never really hurt each other badly, unless by accident. But wrestling got such a violent image that, for a while, the London County Council banned it. Certainly it was not a game for the timid.

I was just a nipper when Dad and Uncle Dick were asked to second one of their first bouts, featuring Jack Pye. The crowd was booing and jeering, and beginning to chuck things themselves, when Jack, sneering and shouting, walked over to the corner and whispered: 'Hit me in the stomach, Jack. Go on, hit me.' Dad, somewhat surprised, obliged, and Jack Pye hung over the ropes, retching, while the punters cheered and clapped. When he recovered he lurched over to Dad, still out of breath, and said: 'Jack, I already know you can hit. But take it easy, you berk. Just make it look good.' After that it became part of the act for Dirty Jack to hit Uncle Dick over the head with a bucket.

There was certainly more niggle in the game in those days, with wrestlers arguing more about who would give a fall to who, how, why and when, and evil promoters who produced blood for the punters by telling one man he would get a fall in round two, then telling his opponent exactly the same thing. Oh dear.

When the public demanded a match between Bert Asseratti and Jack, I heard a story that the two men and the promoter agreed that they should fight a long draw — to give value for money — with Jack getting the first fall. This he duly did, but when the fight re-started, Jack threw a sulk, complaining that the referee had more bias than a crown bowling green, and climbed out of the ring, refusing to fight on.

Jack was disqualifed, naturally, but Bert stalked about blowing fuses, knowing he'd been caught by one of the loveliest cons ever pulled in the game. Jack strutted about for months, saying he'd won really, because he'd got a pinfall against Bert, which was more than Bert had ever managed against him. Jack crowed, and Bert fumed, but he never ever got a fall against Jack.

When I got big, I used this sulking back to the dressing room ploy several times myself, very successfully. Jack was the most brilliant baddy the business has seen. Swanky, conceited, arrogant, lippy and moody, he could make the punters bay for his blood, when really he hadn't done anything very terrible at all. He just made them think he had. Also I respected him because he made himself a huge draw, and a household name, *without the aid of television*. He was a great self-publicist. I remember the papers reporting how he'd done his nut when some suicidal idiot left his bubble car in Jack's very own parking space, outside his Blackpool restaurant. Jack got a hold on the bubble, wrestled it into the middle of the road, and left it there. By some miracle, there was a photographer on the spot to record the event, and, if I remember rightly, another story the following day when the police called to say it wasn't on for him to go around obstructing traffic and blocking the Queen's highway, etc.

When war broke out, I often saw army vehicles on which soldiers had chalked things like: 'Watch out Kraut — Dirty Jack's about', or: 'It's an eye for an eye with Dirty Jack Pye'. So I felt I couldn't do much better than to crib from the best, and much of my own performance was to be influenced by him.

After a year I was confident I'd be accepted into the ranks of wrestlers and, encouraged by the prospect of extra money, at last married my lovely patient Trixie. My mates said it was because I was afraid she'd wear out her engagement ring, so I'd have to buy another. Sadly, only a short time before, my Dad died from heart trouble after a long illness.

I still spent most of my time giving heavyweights sips of water between rounds, but several times I was promoted to the other side of the ropes. I knew all the rules, if you can call them rules, and I had a feel for getting two men working well together (and I mean working up an act), so I wasn't a bad referee. Naturally, I knew who was likely to win. Later I also acted as master of ceremonies at some of my own shows, and had no difficulty in finding enough bullshit to give the boys a good build-up. When I wasn't doing all this, I was pressing weights and wearing out miles of rope by constant skipping.

A year later our son was born. Everybody in the game knows him as J.J. (Jackie Junior) and today he's an excellent wrestler in his own right, and much too good a performer for me to follow. Around about the same time Jackie Dale decided I should give birth to my new career.

When I left his office I was on the books of Dale Martin Promotions. I was a professional wrestler.

SEVEN
THE NEW BOY

THE NEW BOY

My first bout was against a wrestler called Young Atlas, and it seemed I would be allowed one fall. The audience, at Nine Elms Baths, did a lot of yawning, and the promoters must have considered a little encouragement went a long way, for it was four years before I got another fall.

My next appearance was at Exeter, against Cliff Beaumont, a brilliant wrestler, who behaved as if he were a young Alsatian, and I was a rubber ball. He bounced me all over the ring, and I spent much of the time climbing to my feet, while Cliff did backward somersaults, and other smart alec gymnastics, to amuse the crowd. He was not about to make me look good. Lightning fast, he ignored my attempt at a drop kick, quickly side-stepped, and caught me in his arms while I was on the way back down. Bastard.

I was scurfed and screwed by a good many men in those early days, and there were those who had a mean streak and deliberately hurt you just to prove how hard they were. Like Len Brittain's brother, for instance. Formerly a leading amateur, he called himself College Boy, and specialised in kicking your legs from under you. The trouble was he nearly broke your ankles when he did it. Afterwards, if you asked what all the rubbishing was about, the mean men would do their looking-you-straight-in-the-eye bit, and the reply would always be: 'If you don't like it, get a job'.

Though I was 26 years old, and had been connected with the game since I was a youngster, nobody was going to make my apprenticeship an easy one. You had to be hard to get in, and harder to stay in. I daren't speak out of turn or take anything for granted. One night, for example, I turned up early for a show due to start at eight, and by 7.30 p.m. I was sitting in the changing room all ready, with my boots laced up, when the promoter walked in, glared at me, and said: 'What makes you think you're going on bloody first, Pallo? Well, you're not. You're on last.'

Naturally, I thought I'd be on first, as I'd never before

appeared in any other spot, but he was telling me it wasn't on for a new boy to presume anything. I was fresh 'fodder' — wrestling slang that speaks for itself — and wasn't expected to have any initiative. Most shows featured four bouts, occasionally five, with the big faces wrestling second or third (I always preferred second). Fodder always went on first, like a warm-up comedian in variety, and a lot of the punters would still be doing up their flies as I climbed into the ring.

Occasionally a bout would feature two first-class wrestlers — known as 'shooters' — who were no showmen and bored the punters rigid. But fodder that liked to perform a bit, like me, not infrequently closed the show, and eventually this became my regular spot. 'You're on last Jackie, send them home happy,' I'd be told. This I tried to do. If you could produce heat in the last bout, and stop the punters from trickling off to catch the last bus, or get in a pint before closing time, then you were doing all right. Perhaps, in time, you'd even become a 'grafter', a man who worked well, whose performance created heat. A keen grafter studied all the American wrestling magazines, copying and adapting, and would spend hours in the gym, perfecting new moves.

But the grafters, the faces, the clique, were not interested in helping me climb off the fodder heap, and who could blame them? They'd learnt the hard way, so why shouldn't I? Only Stan Stone, a real shooter, Bobby Palmer, Johnny Peters, and Eddie Capelli — the supreme performer at my weight — were prepared to show me a few moves in the gym, and I was grateful to them. However, that came later. For the first two years I learnt by observation, and through my own mistakes. Also, I learnt a lot about class distinction. For the heavyweights ruled. They were the gentry of wrestling, so to speak, and the rest of us were peasants. The heavies topped the bill, always. They always got the best changing rooms, separate from the rest of us if possible, and they sat in the best seats in the motor. If one of the heavy faces shouted: 'Pallo, get my bag from the motor and bring it in here', I'd be off at the trot, because that was the way it was, and because they were all very tasty buggers three times my size.

Heavies got between £8 and £10 a fight, and the really big names, like Asseratti, commanded a bigger screw, while Jack Pye's money was anybody's guess. We welterweights got between £4 to £5 a fight and second best of everything. Seats cost seven shillings and sixpence, (37^{1}/2p), five shillings (25p) half a crown (12^{1}/2p), and, throughout the country, there would always be five shows on somewhere.

Even so, there was never too much work for me. I was earning good money, and I was enjoying it. At noon every day I'd phone Charlie Maskell, the Dale Martin publicity man, to see if illness, injury or whatever, had left any holes in bills which I could fill. I remember doing doubles, for money and a half, if somebody failed to turn up on the night. That meant I'd wrestle twice for £6 if my money for one fight was £4. But I'd never go back in the second time under another name, wearing a mask. Dale Martin weren't out to fool the public in that way. The firm had its own strict rules, and code of ethics, and you didn't wrestle for them unless you conformed.

You were expected to turn up with a good clean towel, good clean boots, good clean gear, and a good clean body. If a bloke was dirty, somebody in the dressing room would always say: 'You pen and ink (stink). Get in the bath.' Everybody else would look at him, and there was never any argument.

Thieving was heavily taboo. Les Martin was with us one night when we went to Swindon. On the way, we stopped for a meal, and when we got to the hall, Les heard this wrestler boasting how he'd half-inched a knife and fork from the café. Les went berserk, and it ended up with us driving up to the café in the early hours of the morning, when no one was about. Then Les made the snitch get out of the truck and post the knife and fork through the letter box.

Most wrestlers are a strange, ruthless, greedy lot (of course I'm including myself), nice guys to work with but not people you'd want to have stay in your house. I can't remember putting up more than two wrestlers overnight in my house, and I haven't got a close wrestler friend. It's typical of the business. Nevertheless, we have our own ways of doing things, our own principles.

For instance, it is unwritten law that you do not make a pass at another wrestler's wife or girlfriend unless you are prepared to have your arms broken by the injured party, enthusiastically helped by everyone else. And if the crowd turns nasty on you as you get out of the ring — as it did with me several times — then you can rely on the other wrestlers to nip out and keep the punters from doing you damage, even if they hate you. And many men hated me when I made it big, because I got my own way and earned a lot more than they did.

I learnt that it was taboo to tell anyone how much you really earned, in case punters wondered why you were prepared to put up with the pain — say of a Boston Crab — for so little. Neither did you talk about the game anywhere in the presence of Joe Public, as someone might earwig and learn some trade secrets.

For this reason outsiders were *never* allowed in the dressing room, however famous they were. If some geezer walked in unexpectedly, a voice would say: 'Queens, queens,' and everybody would stop talking. 'Queens' was short for Queens Park Rangers which, in rhyming Cockney slang, means 'strangers'.

We used a lot of rhyming slang in the ring. If a man muttered 'Me daily,' for example, I knew he meant his back, as 'Daily Mail' equalled 'tail', or back. In the same way there was 'chalk' (Chalk Farm = arm); 'scotch' (scotch peg = leg); 'gregory' (Gregory Peck = neck), and 'plates' (plates of meat = feet). A wrestler's face was his 'boat race', his head was his 'nut' and his nose his 'hooter' or 'trumpet'.

When I got my name up in lights, I used to drive other wrestlers mad by muttering at them through the bout, *my* bout. 'Me daily,' I'd mutter. 'Now me chalk', and if I was laying on my back, say, and hissed, 'Me gregory, me gregory', I'd be prepared for a knee drop on my neck. I've had blokes who've nearly caved my neck in. But a man will only do that once. The word gets around and nobody wants to go in with him.

If a man hit you hard and hurt you, it was 'leady' in wrestling language, and if he had a reputation for being leady, he was a 'leady elbower'. If anybody hits you hard it's called 'potato sacks', and many a time I've told a bloke: 'Hold up, that was a bit potatoes'.

In those early days it was Freddie Unwin, a lovable man, very body building conscious, who taught me something I never forgot. His touch was as light as a feather when we came to grips in a referee's hold — the first contact between two wrestlers — and Freddie smiled at me and said: 'Remember the first law of wrestling, Jackie: "Thou shalt not hurt"'. In time I became known as one of the lightest workers ever in the game. I never inflicted pain unnecessarily. I even heard one promoter say: 'If you've got a broken arm, go in with Pallo and you'll feel no pain'. Incidentally, Freddie was the first man I beat.

In 1952 I built my own car, though I'm damned if I know where I found the time. I welded the chassis out of old girders, and the body from odd pieces of sheet metal. The Pallo Special, painted red, was a two seater, and styled on the lines of a fairground bumper car. She was powered by an ex-War Department Douglas twin generator engine, and when Trixie and I went out in her everybody stopped and made room for us. The Special was a lot of fun to drive and lasted me three years.

Most of my driving, however, was done in the old army trucks which Dale Martin provided to get its men to shows. When these gave their last cough, we graduated to clapped out ex-St John's Ambulances, with dark windows, and finally to an elderly coach, which often ponged horribly from the dead crabs, and other things, which we bloody great schoolboys stuffed in the lining of the roof after performing in seaside towns. You got an extra ten shillings for driving, which was good money, and I grabbed the job whenever possible. After the show I'd drop everybody off near their house, then drive home. In the morning, I'd take the motor to school at St John's Wood, and at lunch time I'd take the truck back to Dale Martin at Brixton.

Other times, I'd be dropped off at Piccadilly in the early hours, and walk down to Charing Cross to wait for a train. The prostitutes were still out in strength in those days, and they'd all shout to each other, and to me.

'Want a good time, dearie?'

'No, ta.'

'Don't bother, luv, he's no good, he's a wrestler. They all want it for nothing, don't they?'

'Well, I don't earn as much money as you do.'

'Wait till somebody tears it off, then you can join the game yourself.'

Chorus of cackles.

'Did you win tonight, dearie?'

'No.'

'Shame. Another crooked bloody match, innit?'

More cackles. I had many a morning chuckle with the ladies of the night, and at that time, a lot of people were getting laughs at my expense. Older wrestlers, like Percy Pitman and Johnny Williams, were always getting me at it. So was Mike Marino, who we called Mick the Fib because he created so much fun out of telling white lies.

I'd go to put on my wrestling boots, and find them nailed to the floor. Or I'd put on my gear and find somebody had emptied a tin of itching powder into it. Watch out, here comes Jack the Scratch.

During long trips, we always stopped for a rest and a stretch. One day Johnny Williams said: 'Come on, let's have a run'. Six of us set off around a field, Johnny beside me, but he started to puff a bit after the second circuit and dropped back. Next time I looked around I was on my own and the ambulance was just disappearing down the road. I ran after it, and every time I caught up and was about to jump in, the bastard driver accelerated and they all fell about laughing. Lou Marco, the old bugger, kept shouting: 'Come on Pallo. Hurry it up. We want to get home.' I must have run about five miles. It kept me very fit.

Driving back from Southampton one night, I was struggling up a steep hill, when suddenly a whacking great truck shot over the top in the middle of the road, making straight at me. I swerved, and Mike Marino, who'd seen what was happening, told everyone to bang on the sides of the motor, which they did. I went spare. Gawd, I'd hit the truck. I stamped on the brakes, and they all started shouting at me that I was a right blind git, had nearly got them all killed and look at the damage I'd done to the motor, and I was screaming that it wasn't me but the lunatic in the truck. When I jumped out to look at the dents, they all wet themselves, and for a moment or two I tried hard to remember exactly what Dad had said about not losing my temper. But I couldn't help smiling. Childish berks.

At Hull Baths, after my bout, I was laying in the tub, shouting to the attendant for more hot water, please, when this geezer in a white outfit walks in with a large bin on his shoulder. I settled back, he heaved the bin over, and next second I'm covered with dog ends, used matches, empty packets, and several things it's best not to mention. Bloody Marino had struck again.

My first taste, or rather sniff, of wrestling humour, came when I was a boy, coming back with my father and a clutch of wrestlers down the old A2. As usual, we stopped to eat, and while we were all noshing, a very large man called Izzy van Dutch walked over to the fire in the corner, bent over as if to warm himself, then walked to the door. Next thing I knew my eyes and nose were stinging and streaming, and something caught at my throat making me cough and splutter non-stop. Everyone else was the same, and we all rushed for the doors. But Izzy was the other side, and he'd slipped one of his gigantic forearms through both door handles, and we couldn't budge him. We coughed and sneezed until he finally let us out, laughing like a bull, and explained that he'd poured two containers of pepper onto the fire. Nice one, Izzy. The last I heard of him he was a postman.

Heavyweight Tony Mancelli had a great sense of humour, and he could tell a good story against himself. One day he is walking down a street in the Elephant and Castle when he sees, coming towards him, a bloke on a cart, loaded with gear, pulled by two horses. Tony steps into the street, puts up his arms so the geezer has to stop, then beckons him down and puts on his posh voice. 'Young man,' he says, 'I'm from the R.S.P.C.A.' and he fishes in his pocket and flashes an official looking piece of paper. Well, the driver is not exactly Mastermind material, so he's worried.

'That horse is lame,' says Mancelli, pointing to the one nearest to him, 'and you'll have to take him back to your depot.' The bloke looks puzzled and says: 'He was all right when I left the yard'. Mancelli frowns and says: 'The point is he isn't now,' and when the driver goes to climb up on his seat he says: 'Just a moment; you'll have to walk them'. The bloke leads the two horses off, muttering something sinister, and it makes Mancelli's day.

Two weeks later Tony walks into the dressing room, the left side of his face bruised black, and he can hardly talk. What happened?

'Tried it again, didn't I,' says Tony, 'and out of all the horses and carts working the Elephant, I have to pick the same one, only this time the bloke was wearing a cap and I didn't recognise him. He just looked at me, smiled, and said: "Once is enough, guv". Then he hit me.'

I believe Tony was there the night of the big Kaluki game — a card game like rummy that we always played in the dressing room while waiting to go on. One of the lads was called to wrestle and asked another bloke to play his hand for him.

When he came back twenty minutes later, the atmosphere was very tense, and his stand-in had got a bloody great pile of money in front of him, and said, 'For Christ's sake don't bother me now, it's all on this hand'. Then the bloke across from him picked up a card, gave a great shout, laid down his hand, and leant over and pulled the big stack of loot towards him. Silence, except for the groans of the loser, who had got his head in his hands. The other geezer was pop-eyed. Suddenly he screamed: 'What the *fuck* did you do that for?', then jumped on the big loser and tried to stomp him into the deck. At which everyone went into hysterics, and they all sat on the bloke and told him there's no need for homicide as he hadn't lost a penny. They'd all pooled their money to give to his stand-in as a joke.

I was driving one night, with Jackie Dale beside me in the front, when we stopped at a café near Dunstable, and the lads climbed out of the back for pie and tea. Jackie and I didn't want any, so we said we'd stay in the motor. Well, they were taking a very long time, and Jackie starts fuming that he wants to get home. He's about to jump out and see what's keeping them, when there's a knock on the window, and a voice with a strong Irish brogue says: 'Would you be giving me a lift to London please?' Jackie glowers and shouts: 'No,' and the Irishman, a large ugly-looking character from what we can see, says: 'For the love of Mary, I'm only asking for a ride'.

'Buzz off,' says Jackie, and at this the Irishman shows that he knows a hell of a lot of old Anglo Saxon and calls Jackie everything. Jackie bellows back that he's going to tear off the Paddy's bogside head, and heaves on the handle of the door to slide it open. The Irishman pulls it shut again, shouting that he wouldn't dirty his hands on the most miserable English pig he's ever met. Jackie, practically foaming, pulls it open again, and the door is going back and fore like a Whitehall farce, with both of them screeching, when the boys come out of the café and start climbing into the back of the ambulance. At this, the Irishman disappears, and the door flies open, nearly doing in Jackie's fingers. He falls out and starts running around the motor, frothing, shouting: 'Where is he?' He looks in the back and asks: 'Where did the bugger go? You must have seen him?' But the boys all look at him as if he's off his rocker, which he nearly was, and say where did who go? Only when they thought Jackie was going to have a seizure did Len Brittain pull a mask out of his pocket, put it on, and say: 'Sure, 'tis foine of you to be giving me a lift, sir'.

I shared a room with Len when we went to Dublin to do an open air show at a football ground. In those days homosexuality was not fashionable, and the word gay still meant happy. So when Len lisps that a nice looking lad like me wouldn't want to sleep alone in a nasty strange town, would he, I start to edge towards the door. Len, a very big lad, smiles horribly and says: 'Come along now and let's have a lovely hot shower together'. I've got my hand on the door handle when he breaks down laughing at the look of fear on my face.

Peter Rann was another one. A hard little bugger with a sardonic, pretty basic sense of humour, very good with the leg pull. For instance, more than once, when we were all dozing on a station platform, we heard a voice shout: 'All right, lads. Train's in. Shift yourselves!' So we'd all tumble aboard and find ourselves going to the wrong place — all, that is, except Peter.

We were on the train to Exeter once, and we had this wrestler with us, fresh over from Australia, who kept saying he was starving and asking if anybody had anything to eat. Peter said all he could offer was chewing gum, and kept bunging him sticks of the stuff. Just before Swindon, he went to the loo, and he was still there at Exeter, when we almost had to prise him off the seat. It was laxative gum, wasn't it, and we were short on the bill that night, because the only thing he could wrestle was a toilet roll.

Naturally, we knew all the best fish and chip shops in the country, and we stopped at one on the way back from Norwich one night. Sammy King, one time promoter who'd been taken over by Dale Martin, was with us as an M.C., and he handed Peter Rann a ten-shilling note. "Ere, Peter, get me some chips.' We'd all finished our nosh, and thought we'd lost Peter, when he came staggering out with half a hundredweight of chips and plonked them on Sammy's lap. 'There you are Sammy,' he said, 'I've put salt and vinegar on for you.' Threepence bought a good portion of chips at that time, and ten bob had bought two complete fry-ups. Sammy was not amused.

Peter was having a drink at the bar in Brighton Ice Rink, having done his stuff, and was watching Lou Marco referee my bout when Lou caught his eye, raised his hand to his mouth and tilted it several times. In anybody's language, that means 'get me a drink', so Peter bought a double Scotch and, finding no water readily available, undid his trousers and produced some himself, adding ice cubes. At the end of the fight he handed it to Lou, who downed it in one.

THE NEW BOY

Several nights later I'm wrestling Peter. I've got him in a hold on the deck, and Lou is leaning over us doing his serious refereeing bit, when Peter begins to chuckle evilly.

'Lou.'

'Whaddya want?'

'Remember that whisky I bought you at Brighton?'

'Yeah, yeah, yeah, so what?'

'Well, I pissed in it.'

I've never seen anybody leave the ring so fast. The punters were understandably baffled, and Peter and I could hardly wrestle on for laughing.

Poor Lou, we used to wind him up something terrible. He got knocked down in the street on his way to the office in Brixton, and his leg was hurt so badly he had to use a stick. Every time he hung it up in the office, someone from the ring crew — the lads who assemble the rings — would nip in and borrow it. Then they'd take the rubber ring off the end, cut half an inch off the stick, and put the ring back on. Every day the stick got shorter and shorter without Lou noticing. I suppose he thought he was shrinking, or something, and it was bloody hard to look at him, and keep a straight face, when he was walking about with this ever diminishing stick. Poor Midget Marco. He got the message when roughly bent double.

In the mid-50s we used to reckon the only chance a wrestler had of getting his picture in the papers was to go to another wrestler's funeral. The promoters said that if a wrestler died, fifty wrestlers would ring up the next day to try to take over his work, and one of the favourite jokes was about two wrestlers standing at the graveside of a fellow pro. As his box is lowered, his wife, mother, father, three sisters and four children all start sobbing loudly.

'Listen to that, Harry,' one wrestler whispers to the other. 'Old Bert never got that sort of heat when he was alive.'

I got to fight Eddie Capelli regularly. And Johnny Peters, Johnny Williams, Percy Pitman, Jack Cusick, Jack Cunningham and many others.

At Streatham, I had a marvellous bout with Stan Stone.

The punters enjoyed it so much they stood up, cheering, and started throwing money into the ring (we call this 'nobbins'), and the M.C. stepped in and geed them up a bit more, so that in the end we collected more than £40 to share out.

Another night — I forget where — only two of us had turned up by the off because it was so foggy. The promoter in desperation told us to wrestle a draw, which meant forty minutes, but to keep demanding another round if we didn't see him wave. He didn't wave until we'd wrestled an hour, and as I was climbing out of the ring, I looked at the audience and saw two of the wrestlers on the bill sitting there. They gave me the thumbs up and big grins, and it turned out they'd been watching us for half an hour without letting anyone know they were there. Rotten shits. But I had to smile when one of them said: 'Gotta keep idle hands busy, lad'.

We were an uncouth crowd of gits, and we did silly, stupid things. But, in the main, we were nice blokes who did our job well and had a lot of fun. The 50s were the happiest years of my wrestling career.

EIGHT
JUST CALL ME 'MR TV'

I remember picking up a paper and reading about an 83-year-old lady whose television set caught fire while she was watching wrestling. She raised the alarm, but the fire spread and half the street had to be evacuated. When all the fuss was over, the first thing she asked was: 'Did Jackie Pallo win?' Now that's what I call stardom.

In the 60s, Pallo became a household name, and I wielded quite a lot of clout inside pro wrestling, which meant I could please my own preferences within reason, and this very much got up the noses of a lot of other fighters. In fact, I became so big it was silly, with tour operators even routing their coaches past my house so it could be pointed out to the passengers.

Everyone knew me as 'Mr TV' Pallo, and at my peak I was driving my SAABs 100,000 miles a year. In a typical week, from Monday to Sunday, I'd drive to Leeds, Rotherham, Sheffield, Morecambe and Edinburgh, returning each night so I could teach school the next morning. Trixie helped me sort out the 600 to 1,000 letters I got every week, mostly from women, and quite a few of them abusive. I always made a point of sending an autographed photograph to those who wrote: 'Don't you dare send me a picture of your rotten, stinking face'. They rarely came back.

I loved being the star. While the other lads travelled all hours, I drove my SAAB, or went first class by train, booking a sleeper for long trips. I'd fly to Edinburgh or Glasgow, and have a hire car waiting so I could drive to Perth, or wherever. I pleased myself and, not surprisingly, jealousy crept — no, galloped — in.

Many wrestlers, particularly the big heavyweights, thought I was a jumped up little twit who got far too much of his own way, and the fact that I was pulling much bigger houses than they were did not improve my popularity. The big maulers really spat blood when I topped the bill at Liverpool, which was unheard of for a lightweight, and it aggravated them that I was on television every five minutes, not just wrestling, but larking about on everybody else's shows, too. But I just raised two fingers and said I'd worked my way up from being the office boy, and now I was going to enjoy the privileges of a top executive, so to speak. I mean, it wasn't as if it had all happened overnight.

I was still trying to climb off the fodder heap, in the 50s, when I decided that pro wrestling could do with some showbiz glamour. It was so bloody dull. Nearly everyone wore the same gear, with either red, blue or green swimming trunks, and I moaned about all this to Joan Rhodes, the strong woman who tied knots in iron bars and things, and is a good mate of mine. She went to Switzerland to do a bit of work, and came back with a pair of striped trunks for me.

That's how it all began, and from then on it snowballed. I chucked away the old dressing gown, and had robes specially made for me with red, blue and mauve mixed with silver, then spangles, and boots sprayed to match. When I first stepped into the groin in my new gear, you could almost hear the eyebrows raising, and everybody sneered and said what a flashy git I was and that it wouldn't last. But now I was known as Gorgeous Jackie Pallo. I dyed my hair blond to add to the image, and eventually sported a pigtail. This wasn't planned. It was just that I was offered a part in a film as an old time sailor, so I had to grow my hair long to get a bow in it. The film sank without trace, but I kept the pigtail as I thought it a good gimmick. It was. I always tied it with a velvet bow, and when I was wrestling four contests a week, Trixie used up two yards of velvet ribbon. At the end of a bout, I'd take off the ribbon and throw it to one of the ladies who'd given me a real slagging off. They loved it.

By then I was 'wrestling's favourite bad man' or 'the man you love to hate', a flash, arrogant, cocky bighead who fought dirty and screamed at the punters. Unfortunately, I was so convincing that a lot of people in the game came to believe that I was really like that, and I remember Les Martin looking at me funny one day and saying: 'I've created a bloody monster'. Les, of all people. Silly git, he could have really upset me. But I forgive him, for it was Les who tagged me 'Mr TV'.

That year I was asked to do a little bit on 'Sunday Night at the London Palladium', which was the biggest television show of the era. Don Arrol was the resident comedian-cum-master of ceremonies, and I had to fake up some wrestling and scurf him about for a giggle. At the rehearsal, I went on with Peter Cockburn, who said he wanted all the folk to meet Jackie Pallo, the wrestler. I interrupted, and said: 'No, introduce me as Mr TV'. Uncertainty from Cockburn, silence from the other watching artistes, and then, from the blackness at the back of the hall a voice called: 'OK'. Cockburn looked relieved, and that night millions of TV viewers heard me called 'Mr TV' for the first time. I've always believed that the voice from the back was that of Val Parnell. A big thanks to him if it was, because overnight I became the biggest thing in wrestling since the invention of the wheel.

Barbara Hutton was the star that night, and the following week it was Lena Horne. I went back for a chat with Don and stayed to watch her. Great. I loved the Palladium.

'63 was a vintage year. There were about 600 pros — many of them part-timers — taking part in at least 100 promotions a week, and wrestling was voted the biggest spectator 'sport', which caused not a few of us to smile as we held out our hands for the money. It was always in the top ten of the television TAM ratings, and soon became an even bigger draw than two of the most popular shows of the day — 'Z Cars' and 'Dr Finlay's Casebook'. More than half the fans were women, and on the train I met a nice man called Cohen. He ran Tescos and he blamed me especially for keeping several million ladies glued to their sets on Saturdays when they should have been out spending their money in his stores.

'Remember "Dick Barton, Special Agent"?' he said. 'Well, everybody used to stay in and listen to that on the radio. You're television's Dick Barton.'

A few days later I read that Tom Lynch, secretary of the National Union of shopkeepers, was writing to ITV to ask them to put on something less popular than wrestling on Saturdays as his members were losing a lot of money and it was a 'serious matter'. What a bloody hope.

JUST CALL ME 'MR TV'

On 22 May 1963 Prince Philip made the game respectable by turning up to watch a televised charity show at the Royal Albert Hall, and shook hands with me, Mick McManus, Tibor Szakacs, Joe Cornelius, Johnny Kwango, Steve Logan, Bert Royal and Billy Robinson, and said he was sorry he was late, but we knew how it was.

Les Martin fluttered around, very nervous, before the off, telling all of us he'd have our guts for garters, and that we'd never work again (yawn) if any of us dared to go out of the ring and land within five miles of the duke. This was because the press photographers were offering good money to anyone who'd land in the prince's lap without actually crippling him. I was offered £20 myself, but I said, come, come, no way. I was wrestling Johnny Kwango, and I decided to throw him to the duke instead. Naturally, I didn't tell Johnny, and nobody was more surprised when I suddenly chucked him over the top rope. He caught hold with one hand, but I hammered this until he let go and landed at the duke's feet. He was sick as a parrot, but much happier when he saw his picture in the paper. I should have charged him a fee.

The prince's blessing on the old grunt and groan meant that we got a different class of people watching. I mean, the upper crust wouldn't be seen dead at the back in Poplar Baths, shouting: 'Fucking give him one,' or, 'Tear his bloody balls off', but it was all right for them now to book a booth and booze and laugh and enjoy it as the in thing to do. Jolly funny, these fellas, what?

Prince Philip gave me a big grin and said he saw I was still wearing ribbon in my hair, and I was tempted to say that it wasn't everyone who had enough hair to do this. But I thought of Les Martin. He was too young to die of apoplexy. I'd watched the duke closely during the bouts, and he did a lot of laughing, which you don't do if you are bored. He came to another charity show at the Albert Hall the following year, and I think we might have had a regular punter there. Whatever, he certainly gave the business a big boost.

But, of course, it was television that made it. My first appearance on the box was with Joan Rhodes, at the show to celebrate the first anniversary of commercial TV. I let her Irish Whip me to show viewers just how tough a good-looking strong woman could be. Hughie Green and Mr and Mrs Smith's Five Little Boys were on the same bill, and it all took place at a Piccadilly Hotel. George 'Chuck' Sewell, actor friend of my Islington youth club days, was earning a few bob there as a waiter, not knowing he'd be picked to star in the 'Special Branch' TV series. We had a beer together.

The big day arrived when Joint Promotions announced that they had signed a contract to stage wrestling as part of ITV's Saturday sports coverage, and a lot of the lads began looking to their profiles, from the belly upwards, in preparation for 'take one'. The contract was rumoured to be worth £15,000 a week, which is very healthy when you consider that wrestlers were only being paid £25 at first, and later £40 for a TV stint, even in the early 70s. The most ever I got was £80 for a Cup Final day fight, and that was only because I did such a lot of heavy moaning.

Anyway, you'll remember that Joint Promotions still has the wrestling contract for 'World of Sport' on Saturdays, and at that time put on 4,500 odd fights a year in halls all over Britain, which was 95 per cent of the action. Joint was a kind of alliance between the main promoters, who decided it was better to work together than kick each other in the teeth, as in that way they could produce a lovely big cake, and cut it into nice big slices. More money for all, except perhaps the wrestlers, because Joint Promotions, having a stranglehold (or, perhaps, Full Nelson) on the game, were in a position to dictate the sort of money they wanted to pay. After all, who else could you work for apart from a handful of cowboys? The only other independent promoter of any size was Paul Lincoln, an Australian who wrestled as Dr Death, who had a contract with Granada Cinemas to stage wrestling shows. And he couldn't employ all that many.

Joint put on the best wrestling, and all the promoters retained their separate identities in their own areas. The alliance was often an uneasy one, as it involved some men who did not get on, to put it mildly.

In the south there was Dale Martin, which was Les Martin and the Dale brothers (real name Abbey), Jackie, Johnny and Billy. Norman Morrell, a former British Olympic representative, and Ted Beresford operated out of Yorkshire, and there was Billy Best in Liverpool and Arthur Wright of Wryton Promotions in Manchester. Also up north were George de Relwyskow, and Arthur Green, the secretary of Joint, and all this lot used to meet up once a month at Kirkgate Chambers, Leeds, to decide which wrestlers would fight where and for whom.

Max Crabtree, who now runs Joint Promotions under Billy Dale, and who attended many of the meetings, told me that my name was invariably the first out of the hat, and they'd decide my fighting fixtures for the next month. 'Right George, you have Pallo for four days, then Billy has him for the next four,' and so on. Each promoter would send out to the wrestlers on his books a list of dates, times and places, and off we'd all trot. Occasionally, promoters would be interviewed after meetings and say how mad they got when people suggested fights could be fixed, and that they, and the boys who fought for them, wrestled clean and straight. Just like we all said.

The directors of Joint were a little concerned in the mid-60s when it was announced that the Monopolies Commission might investigate the game, though they all said they had nothing to fear. The whole thing came to nowt. Sir John Langford-Holt, Conservative MP for Shrewsbury, asked the Postmaster General in 1965 to ban TV 'bogus wrestling' contests which were calculated to deceive the public. A few months later he called the shows 'rehearsed charades' and asked the Minister of Sport to set up a Board of Control for wrestling, just like that of boxing. The minister said it wasn't his responsibility, and Les Martin stepped in bravely and said Joint Promotions were setting up their own nationwide board which would require every pro wrestler to be licensed. The same year the Variety Artistes Federation welcomed all wrestlers as members, but two years later when it merged with Equity, the boys were chucked out. I wasn't, because I was making legitimate stage appearances in pantomime and that, and had been a member of Equity since 1960.

But back to the TV contract. It is not generally known that Cliff Beaumont and I were the first two wrestlers to appear before the ITV cameras. Unfortunately they were not broadcasting at the time. The camera crews needed a dress rehearsal for the first show, so Cliff and I went down to Westham Baths, and Cliff threw me about for an hour while the camera boys experimented with different angles.

About a week before, I met an actor, Kent Walton, at Rochester, and Mike Marino and me were asked to sit beside him and tell him what the boys were doing to each other in the groin. We got on well, and at the first live show, there I was sitting beside Kent as technical adviser, as it were. He asked if I could do it on a permanent basis, while he learned his trade, and Dale Martin agreed and paid me a small fee. I did that for about 18 months, and by then there wasn't any wrestling jargon Kent didn't know. He was even making up names himself for new moves. He always had a good imagination, and he needs it today when he's watching mountains of fat who do nothing except belly butt each other.

I became very friendly with Kent, and he was quite shattered when J.J. told him I was leaving Dale Martin to start up on my own. I always have a chuckle when I hear him rattling on about what a very sporting bout it is, and how nice it is to see so much handshaking. 'Oh beautiful,' he says. 'Now he's starting on the back weakeners. What a beautiful spin out. I do hope we don't start on the forearm smashes as early as this. That caught him unawares. He looks aghast at the ease with which his opponent did that. He's going for the same hold, and yes . . . yes . . . he's got it!' Good old Kent. I hope he goes on for ever.

While I was working with him I watched the camera crews and got to know a lot about the angles. It stood me in good stead later, as I always knew where the cameras were pointing when I was in the groin, and I worked to them, timing my stunts carefully. But at one time, it looked as though I was going to become 'Mr ex-TV'. I was called aside and told that people had complained about my violent, villainous fighting, and that the junta didn't want me frightening families to death while they sat in front of the fire in their living rooms. It seems bloody daft when I think of the extent of violence shown on television today, but in those days everybody believed it was for real when you stepped on a geezer's nose and spun around. Well, almost everybody.

But by now I was putting a lot of arses on seats, and I didn't intend to change my style. Eventually, they saw the light, and after that I probably made more appearances on the box than any other wrestler. In a manner of speaking, I was on TV every week, because every time the credits came up the viewers could see me and Alan Dennison.

Television was very good for us lightweights because camera angles made big and small men look roughly the same size on the screen. Comparatively small men, like Mick McManus and me, could be made to look like giants, and a lot of people were surprised to discover we were not enormous when they met us face to face. For instance, when actor John Gregson, who was quite a big man, first met Mick he said: 'Here, you're a midget'.

And, of course, this equalising effect of the cameras meant that the big heavies could no longer lord it over the rest. Class distinction was abolished, and there was a lot of scowling.

In the 60s I wrestled quite a lot in Spain, and several times in France. I went to Spain for the fun of it, and for a free holiday for me, Trixie and J.J. The pay was nothing — about a tenner a time — but the atmosphere was terrific. I always topped the bill, and you could be wrestling in front of 100,000 people. The promoters even put chairs on the sand of the bullring itself, and when I looked up from the groin I could see a myriad pinpoints of light from the cigars and cigarettes. J.J. would sit beside Trixie, blinking to keep awake so he wouldn't miss me, as the shows normally didn't start until eleven at night. By the time I got into the ring, its surface was sprinkled with sand, carried in on the feet of the wrestlers who'd gone before me, and this could rub away your skin, and was very painful if I'd got sunburned during the day.

The Spaniards screamed and hollered and loved every second of it. In Barcelona and Valencia I was carried from the bullring and chaired through the streets, with thousands cheering and waving. A fantastic experience.

At one town, where I wasn't fighting, I called in to the dressing room see the boys who were performing and said hullo to everyone except the bloke in the corner. He said: 'Don't you want to talk to me then?' and I said: 'Certainly, but I don't know you, do I?' He fell about laughing. 'You berk,' he said, 'we've been together a hundred times.' Turned out it was Kendo Nagasaki (a tough English lad called Peter), and this was the first time, in the years I'd known him, that I'd ever seen him without his mask. Peter really lived the part. He even showered with his bloody mask on, and we used to kid on that he must have the dirtiest face ever.

I only remember one unpleasant incident in Spain. An American woman threw a Coke bottle into the ring — no great crime — and the Spanish police, in their funny hats, dragged her from her seat and started lambasting her with their big sticks, making a right mess of her face. I jumped up to go and help, but one of the Spanish wrestlers got a head lock on me and made it plain that they'd beat me to pulp if I interfered. The police, that is. They do get carried away over there.

Back home, if I wasn't wrestling on the box, I was appearing on other people's shows. Dozens of them. My first TV acting part was on 'Emergency Ward 10', when they featured an outpatients' unit and I was the wrestler who came in with a broken coccyx which, for those without dictionaries, is the bone at the bottom end of the spine. News of my appearance got around, and on the Friday that 'Emergency Ward 10' was screened, there were only about three people in the hall at Northampton, where I was wrestling, when the first bout was due to start. Jackie Dale panicked until somebody told him that all the punters were watching me do my bit on the box. He put back the start by half an hour, and as soon as my coccyx was fixed, the hall filled up. Jackie said he'd never known anything like it happen before, and not to let it go to my head.

JUST CALL ME 'MR TV'

A few years later and I was in 'The Avengers', as a gravedigger who had to wrestle with Honor Blackman, playing Cathy Gale, for possession of a spade at the edge of an open grave. Now it's not everyone who has wrestled with Honor Blackman, so I forgive her for letting go of the bloody spade while I wasn't expecting it, so that I fell into the grave and knocked myself out. As a result, a Greek called Vassily Mantoupolos had to forgo the pleasure of fighting me at Southend, poor fellow. Twelve years later, in 1976, I fell into the orchestra pit while struggling with John Warwick, a singer, who was rehearsing with me for my part as Bad Baron Heinke, in *Goldilocks and the Three Bears* at Barnsley. You could say I have specialised as the Bad Baron. He was my first role when I began in pantomime at Norwich in 1969 and, though I played Ebenezer in *Aladdin*, at Hull, and an ugly sister in *Cinderella*, London, the Bad Baron is my favourite. I've played five to ten week runs in pantomime for 16 consecutive years now, and hope to go on (always as a baddie, of course) for many years.

In 1971 I was approached by an outfit who were staging Prokofiev's *Peter and the Wolf* at the Royal Albert Hall, and thought it would be a brilliant idea for me to be the narrator. Until they mentioned it, I didn't know what the hell it was, but I agreed, probably because the money was so good, and learned the whole thing off by heart. On the night, they put me in the same dressing room that Sir Malcolm Sargent, and gawd knows how many other famous conductors had used, and just before the off, somebody came in and said it wasn't a very good house, but not to worry.

I thought this meant the place might be half full, but when I walked across the stage to the rostrum, it took me several minutes to spot anybody at all. Later I was told that there were about 500 people rattling around inside, so it was not a successful venture. Funny really, as not many weeks before I'd wrestled there, and it was so full that 50 people fell out every time somebody opened a door. Still, I was pleased with my performance, and I had a good laugh when the manager told me he'd had to refund the money to an elderly couple who thought me and J.J. were fighting another tag team called Peter, and The Wolf.

I made a record called 'Everyone Should Get What I've Got', written for me by Les Reed, and recorded by the Chapter One Record Co., and it may be that there are still a few people alive who've heard it. One of the main reasons it didn't do well is that I'm a lousy singer, but it might have done better if the BBC hadn't been wetting its knickers about record plugging at the time.

With Trixie (who's got a good voice) and J.J., I made another record. The three of us sang some forty songs, backed by a choir, including 'Maybe It's Because I'm a Londoner', which was called 'Ring-a-Long With The Pallos', and was also several noughts short of winning a golden disc.

My T-shirts, with Mr TV emblazoned over a colour picture of me on the front, lost money, but I think I was about ten years early bringing them out. But I did make a lot of loot advertising on TV a very well-known electric razor, and an equally well-known gravy browning. I was also paid a lot for wandering around impersonating the founder of a brewery, advertising a new beer, looking an idiot in funny shoes and a long, velvet-collared coat, with my hair curled and crimped to look like an old time wig.

I was dressed like this one day when I tottered into the bar of the Carlton Hotel, in Great Yarmouth, where I was staying, and bumped into Des O'Connor, who had also booked in. He looked at me and nearly got a hernia laughing. And he wouldn't believe that the hair was really mine until he'd tugged it hard. Cheeky bugger.

I made more money putting my name to a strip in the old *Evening News*, London, aimed at teaching their readers how to wrestle, and, all in all, the old bank balance wasn't doing too badly. Payments varied, but at some halls I was getting £120 a show, and there were £150s and £250s too. The most I ever got was £600 for a contest against Mick McManus at the Albert Hall, when they doubled the prices and sold every seat.

It was seven days a week living in those days. If I wasn't doing daft things on television shows, I was opening

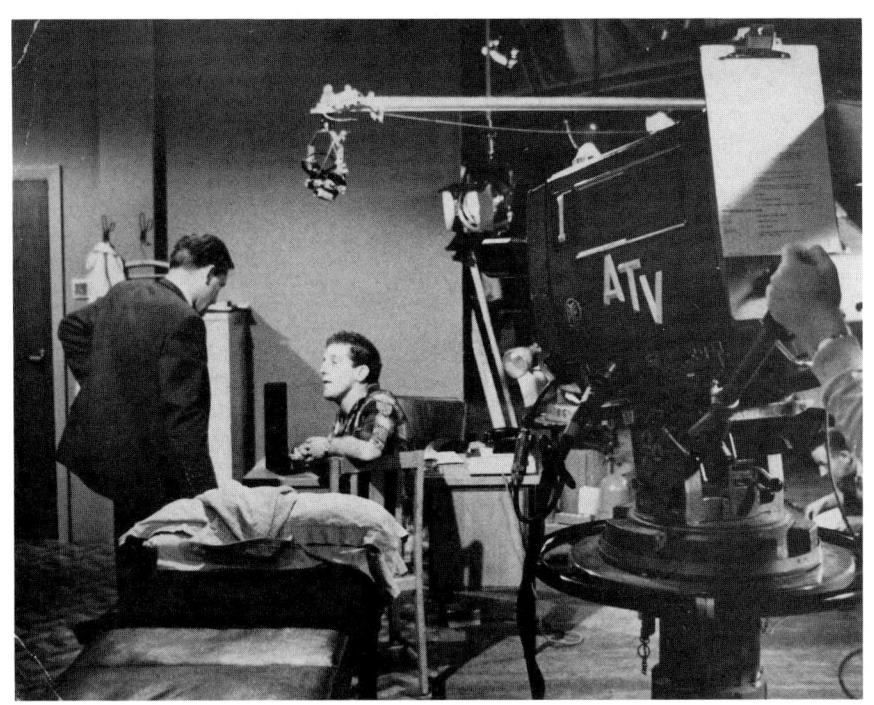

Television star — in 'Emergency Ward 10'...

...and with Honor Blackman in 'The Avengers'.

Pantomime villain — Bad Baron Heinke in Goldilocks and the Three Bears.

Photographed for the cover of 'Ring-a-Long with the Pallos' with Jackie Junior and Trixie.

Jackie in the lions' cage at Gerry Cottle's Circus.

Promoter Pallo discusses a programme with his M.C.

OVERLEAF:
Jackie 'Mr TV' Pallo.

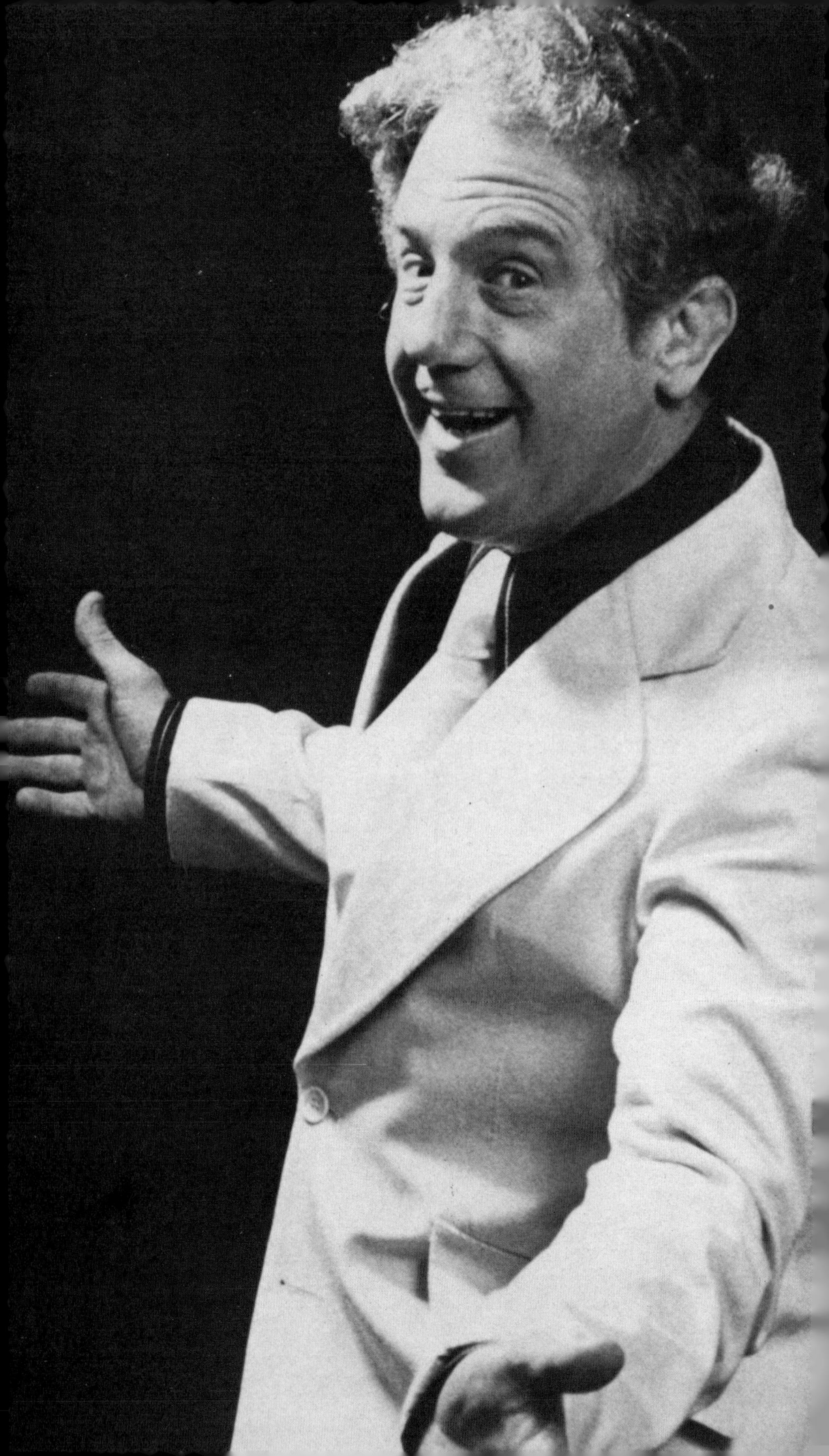

something, or judging beauty contests and picking glamorous grannies. I played charity darts, football and cricket, and was good at going around with a bucket and getting the crowd to chuck money into it. When I played against the Bunny Girls at football, four of them jumped on me and ran away with my pants. I should be so lucky again. For a long time, I played with Colin Cowdrey's cricket team of celebrities, which raised a lot of money for charity. I became very friendly with Freddie Trueman. Freddie knew that people came along to see twits like me hitting the ball at least once or twice, so he'd let me have six balls to lash out at, then he'd say: 'Don't hit this one, lad,' and down would come a ball I never even saw, which invariably took out the middle stump. My greatest moment on the team was when Sir Len Hutton came up to me, pumped my hand, and said how pleased he was to meet me. He wasn't half as pleased as I was. I was sorry when I had to give up the team, but I was involved in so many goings-on that Trixie and I never had time to relax together. So, something had to go.

We went to Dartmoor, Trixie, J.J. and me, with Aimi Macdonald and Lionel Blair and his dancers, to put on a show for the prisoners. We were in panto at Torquay at the time. So Aimi sang; I sang (to a captive audience!); and Lionel and his lot did their bit, and then J.J. and I walked onto this makeshift ring they'd put up. I said: 'You dirty rat,' and he said: 'Dad, this is for real,' and off we went. Then I tried something ambitious. There was an almighty crack and the whole ring collapsed in a huge cloud of dust. The cons thought it was hilarious. The Scots bloke who made tea for us was still chuckling when he poured it. I asked him what he was in for, and he said murder. Seems he had chinned a fella in Glasgow and killed him. He was a nice bloke.

A few years later, J.J. was in prison again, at Chelmsford nick, where he had a titchy part in the film *Porridge*. One of the real screws showed J.J. the execution room. Someone had put up a long piece of string with a noose at the end of it for a laugh. Great sense of humour.

Of course, publicity always helped, and there are two stunts we did which I recall vividly.

I went along to Gerry Cottle's Circus, near Slough, wearing my white satin cabaret-act suit (yes, that's right, I do cabaret, too), and the press lads took pictures of me with my head under the foot of a six ton elephant. No trouble, piece of cake. Then everybody said what a marvellous picture it would make if I went into the lions' cage and did a bit of taming. Fine. I like cats, and lions, after all, are just big cats.

The trainer was known as Uncle Arthur, and when I went into this cage with him, it was empty. Then there was a noise like a miniature stampede, the cage began to shake, and down the metal tunnel came these five great monsters, looking very unhappy. Arthur had hold of my hand, and he said: 'Just keep calm, and stay where you are'. I wasn't about to move, especially as one of the monsters brushed my arse as they ran round and round. Arthur barked an order, and they all lay down in front of us, 18 inches away. Right before me was a lioness called Lulu, who was eyeing me as if she wondered whether I'd be better with or without Worcester sauce.

All the press photographers are shouting for me to move around a bit and do this, and do that, and I'm telling them what they can do. Arthur hands me a white walking stick, and says I'm to tell Lulu to go back. 'Point it at her,' he says. I do. 'Back,' I squeak. Like a flash, Lulu paws the stick with her left and sends it flying. 'She won't go back,' I whisper, beginning to think my white suit is going to turn brown. 'Back!' roars Arthur, and as Lulu edges back, looking very nasty, I watch the claws of her front paws leave deep tracks in the grass. Obviously the lions know that I have lost my bottle. So does Arthur. 'Stand behind me,' he mutters, 'and back very slowly towards the door of the cage.' I back, sweat running down my face. When I got to the door I was gone. 'Just get me out of this fucking cage,' I said.

Arthur took me back to his caravan, produced a bottle of whisky, and showed me the scars on his body, made by lions, while I was drinking about half of it. The trouble, he says, is that the lions were nervous. They are not used to being asked to perform first thing in the morning, and they didn't like the silence. They were used to noise, lights, people and the sounds they make. He took me to watch the lions feed. Each was gnawing a cow's head fresh from the abattoir, and it wasn't hard to visualise a blond head with a pigtail amongst them. I wished he had fed them before I made my entrance.

None of the papers used a picture of me with the lions. They printed the one of the elephant not standing on my head, though there's lots of people who wish it had. A few weeks later Lulu put a few more nasty scars on Arthur's body.

The only other elephant I met was a baby, about a tenth the size of the first one, who was running around in a lovely animal sanctuary, near Stirling, in Scotland. The sanctuary's publicity man thought it would be a good chuckle if half a dozen wrestlers had a tug of war with the baby elephant, so I went along, with J.J., three Scots lads, and our own baby elephant, Giant Haystacks, as anchor man. We were all introduced to the baby, stroked his trunk and said what a nice little fellow he was, and that it was a pity he stood no chance. Then the keeper put a rope around his neck, we took the strain at the other end of it, and the press boys lined up for their pictures.

We sweated, we heaved. The elephant looked at us kindly and moved not an inch. Nearby there was a tree stuffed full of monkeys, and they must have thought this funny, as they all started screaming. Suddenly the elephant reared up on his hind legs, pulling all six of us towards him, and straight away we all lost our bottle and dropped the rope. The elephant trotted off, trailing the rope, and it promptly caught in the wheel of the Transit van, in which we'd arrived, so that the van took off too, sideways.

Then the little jumbo changed his mind and turned back to charge at us. Panic. Somebody shouted: 'The tree, the bloody tree,' and we all started running around the trunk of this tree with jumbo, now free of the Transit, chasing us and waving his trunk. I never knew Haystacks could move that fast. The keeper was shouting, and the monkeys, obviously very frightened, all started letting go from both ends, so that after several circuits we were covered in piss and crap. Eventually, the elephant got fed up with us, and the monkeys, and walked off, smirking, with his keeper. Frankly, I preferred the one that didn't stand on my head. I didn't fancy giving Haystacks the kiss of life.

My son, Jackie, was booked by Arthur Wright to fight his first bout at Shrewsbury, on 21 June 1971.

Of course, I'd been wrestling with Jackie ever since he was old enough to toddle, just playing about, and he'd naturally picked up quite a lot from me. He'd been part of the wrestling scene ever since he was eight years old, but originally he wanted to go into showbusiness, probably due to my influence, as I was always yattering about it.

So he got a job as dresser to Brian Rix, in the West End's Garrick Theatre, then moved on to become an assistant stage manager, or glorified tea boy, at £12 a week. He had a lot of fun, learned a lot about the stage, but thought he might well die of malnutrition if he didn't earn a bit more money.

He started coming to some shows with me, towards the end of the 60s, and met several wrestlers' sons who were just starting in the game, following in their fathers' footsteps, and decided to follow mine. I was a big star, and Jackie Dale could easily have made a lot of money out of the lad by insisting on launching him straight away, billing him as the second sensational Pallo, and such bullshit. But Jackie Dale was not like that and, with my full approval, told J.J. to spend a year at the Brixton HQ gym, learning how to wrestle.

J.J. joined what the rest of us called the Sunday Morning Boys, the amateurs who wanted to become pros, who were taught by Bernard Murray. They should have called him 'Professor' Murray, because what Bernard didn't know about wrestling could have been engraved on the head of a pin. A master. He was a lovable, bald-headed little Yorkshireman, and if you saw him in the street when the traffic was heavy, you'd probably ask him if he wanted seeing across the road.

But in the groin Bernard was vicious, and could scurf and screw shooters three times his size. However he could only give them half the act, so to speak. He couldn't teach them how to perform, how to put arses on seats. You can't supply personality.

I remember a reporter from Fleet Street, who'd been a bit of an amateur, coming to the gym to write a story with me about wrestling. When he got there they told him sorry, but Jackie Pallo was working that night and couldn't be tired out. Would he like to have a go with a couple of the up-and-coming men? Certainly. Well, they tossed and dragged the poor fellow all over the place, and after he recovered he limped over to talk to me. 'If those lads are the learners,' he said, 'then it's a damn good job I didn't wrestle with you.' He didn't know he'd been in with a couple of the top shooters.

After a while J.J. became my tag partner. Now there are quite a few fathers and sons in the game, but previously they'd always billed the son as a younger brother, so that the old man wouldn't look *too* old. But I wanted Pallo and Son, and I got it. Initially, it was a good idea for J.J. to go into tag, because it gave him time to get over his nerves and develop his timing and professionalism. When he made mistakes there were three others to cover for him, including his dad, and it wasn't long before we were packing halls all over the country.

The really big tag match was to be Pallo and Son versus Mick McManus and Steve Logan. Villains all. The gee-up went on for months, with Mick always mentioning it in his newspaper column and saying what horrible things were going to happen to the Pallos, and the four of us had a try out, a sort of dress rehearsal for the event, at the Sophia Gardens Pavillion, Cardiff. Then everybody started blowing trumpets — THE TAG MATCH THE WRESTLING WORLD HAS BEEN WAITING FOR — tarraaaa! at the Royal Albert Hall, on Wednesday 31 May 1972. Posters went up with our pictures all over them (theirs were bigger than ours: the Office Hold again), seat prices were doubled, ranging from 25p for somewhere up in the roof to £3.50, and the place was sold out. Also on the bill were Tibor Szakacs, Steve Vidor, Adrian Street, Kendo Nagasaki and Mike Marino. Me and J.J. in fact lost, but the punters got good value, and everybody went home happy. I believe they paid J.J. £50. He got more than that selling three tickets we'd left for friends who didn't turn up.

J.J. has never looked back. He's inherited all my

showmanship, and added quite a few new tricks of his own. Like me, he wears a pigtail, and elderly wrestlers are always creaking up to me and saying, huskily: 'Saw Junior last night, Jackie. It was like turning back the clock twenty years and watching you again.' Silly old buggers; do I need reminding?

Unfortunately the business itself was declining — I mean, the way in which it was being run — and in a way I felt that I might have contributed towards this. Not that I meant to, but there you are.

It was like this. One night, pushing the 70s, Jarvis Astair, the millionaire sporting entrepreneur (I think he's called), took me aside after he'd been up to watch a match in which I'd taken part. He said he was interested in the possibility of buying the firm of Dale Martin, and was I willing to give him any information. I said yes. I couldn't see any harm in it. I said Jackie and Les knew all there was about running the game and the outfit was thoroughly straight. Anyway, my information may have helped him make up his mind to make his sucessful takeover bid for Dale Martin, and there was a lot of talk at the time that the deal was conditional on me and Mick McManus being on the books.

During the next few years, Astair took over Wryton Promotions (Arthur Wright had more or less retired at the time), plus Billy Best and Norman Morrell and Ted Beresford. He also bought out Paul Lincoln, who soon went back to Australia, and that only left George de Relwyskow — an ex-wrestler who I liked a lot — and Arthur Green, together with Max Crabtree, who worked with them when he wasn't working for himself. Max was another ex-wrestler.

So Jackie, Les, Norman, Ted and Billy retired, robbing the game of five of its top men. Arthur Green had left Joint, and in a few years poor old George died.

Billy Dale was put in at the top, and his brother Johnny, who'd been managing director at the time of takeover, was overshadowed. In time, Astair sold out to Sears Holdings, part of the William Hill Group, but as of now, Billy Dale is still running things, and Max Crabtree is masterminding Joint Promotions.

Anyway, after the takeover, they brought in a bloke called Mike Judd, who'd been sort of general dogsbody for Paul Lincoln, and made him a director to run Dale Martin wrestling under Billy Dale. Disaster. People resented the way in which he gave orders and seemed to expect everyone to run around after him. Some of the new lads were quite willing to hover, banging their foreheads on the floor when the word came down from Judd, but J.J. — who'd been around wrestling for 13 years and was accepted as one of the family — was not amongst them. The only forehead he was likely to bang on the floor was Mr Judd's, and I felt the same.

I felt that Judd should never have been put in a position where he could tell experienced wrestlers what to do. He even tried to tell *me* what falls to do and how to do them. I was, I swear, momentarily lost for words. 'How fucking dare you?' I then said. 'Don't you tell me how to graft.' He may as well have told Renoir how to paint. Once I walked into the office in Brixton, which I'd been doing for a quarter of a century, and he looked up, and said very nastily: 'I didn't hear you knock'. He was so sarcastic that I had him up against the wall and was about to demonstrate what would happen if he ever spoke to me like that again, when Mick McManus intervened and calmed me down. Full marks to Mick on that occasion. Pity, though. J.J. also had him up against a wall over an argument about money. And we weren't the only ones.

Now, my schedule was booked for months ahead, and I can understand the office getting a bit irritated with people ringing up for me constantly, asking about bits in films, plays, or TV chat shows, or quizzes, or pantomimes. But my popularity was good for them, too. It was certainly keeping the halls jammed to busting. So there were times when I wondered why they'd tried so hard to block my interview with Bernard Braden, for instance, and if it was really necessary for me to turn down film parts because they wouldn't release me. Even when I played Barbara Windsor's husband in the film *Not Now Darling*, I left the set at 5 p.m. so I could motor to Weymouth to wrestle. This I didn't mind. Unlike others, I *never* let the punters down. If I didn't turn up, I was really ill.

Mick McManus used to say to me: 'You've got to make up your mind whether you want to make wrestling or showbusiness your living'. There was truth in what he said, but it seemed to me that the two worlds were closely connected, and that there were people in the office who were frequently going out of their way to make life harder for me.

What particularly soured me was the story behind the 'This is Your Life' programme, which Eamonn Andrews sprang on me in April 1973. But J.J. knows a lot more about that than I do, so let him tell it in his own way.

'Well, naturally, I had to be in on it from the start [J.J. talking], and so did Dale Martin. Half the wrestling world had been sworn to secrecy, and I was working closely with Malcolm Morris, the producer, and his researchers. They'd done the whole thing, contacting everybody who knew Dad from the year dot, and they'd arranged to fly in people from all over the place.

'Everything was set up to take place at the Fairfield Hall, in Croydon, where Dad was topping the bill, and Malcolm Morris had arranged to have the cameras in all the right places, so that it looked like the show was being filmed for 'World of Sport', and would go out on Saturday.

'I couldn't believe it when I got a call from a shattered Malcolm Morris to say that Dale Martin had been on the phone to say sorry, but Dad wouldn't be available at Croydon as they'd switched him to perform at Aberdeen instead. Well, I went completely spare. I wasn't having Dad buggered about like that. I told Malcolm Morris that if he had any more trouble with the office he must let me know, and I would hire a hall and book the wrestlers myself.

'I got on to the office and told them they must be off their bloody heads, that it had cost the TV company several thousand pounds to cancel, and that I would be very upset indeed if they decided to scrap the whole thing. Some idiot told me that you had to treat TV people like that, otherwise they would think they only had to snap their fingers to get people to do what they wanted. By that time I was practically eating the phone.

'In the end it was done at Reading, about three months later. Dad was due to wrestle Adrian Street in the final bout, and as soon as the introductions were done, in nipped Eamonn Andrews.

'Billy Dale was very cold to me at the party following the programme, but it was Dad's big night, so I said nothing. I was just grateful that the TV company had decided to go ahead. I didn't tell Dad what had happened until some time after.'

And when J.J. told me, it did not make me any happier with the set-up.

On the night the show was screened, I had driven all the way to Perth for a show. I dived into a hotel and said quick, where's the TV lounge, as I must see' This Is Your Life', 'cos I'm on it. I switched on, and Eamonn was just saying: 'Jackie Pallo, this is *your* life,' when a drunken Scot flopped into the seat next to me and bent my ear, at ten thousand decibels, all the way through the programme, between sips from a hip flask. He wouldn't shut up, and I can't lip read, so it was a bit like looking at a silent movie. Still, they tell me it had the highest rating of all the programmes that week.

After that things got steadily worse between J.J., me, and Judd. If I questioned him about anything, his stock answer was: 'If you don't like it, do something else'.

So I did.

One morning in 1975 I telephoned Judd, told him to cross me and J.J. off the books at the end of the week, and hung up before he'd finished spluttering. I'd decided to become a promoter. J.J. and me would wrestle in our own shows.

I called myself Pallo Enterprises — The Star Who Presents The Stars.

NINE
THE GODFATHER

However, it was not long before everybody in the game was calling me the Godfather, and I like to think it was because I was making some of them cash offers they couldn't refuse. Anyone who suggests anything different will be receiving a visit. That's a joke.

Certainly I seemed to end up on the receiving end of some naughty tricks. I learned that promoting has a lot of pitfalls, and I fell into most of them. But into some I felt I was pushed, and when I'm pushed, I tend to shove back.

My problem was that I always tried to play the gentleman when it came to business, and by the time I discovered that this didn't work, it was too late. I'd lost a great deal of money. In the beginning, I was so naive that I thought there'd be no aggro. Wasn't there enough room in the business for everybody to make money? Why not live and let live with jolly Jack Pallo?

If I did someone a good turn, they, naturally, would do one for me. Some hope. So, at the end of my first show, at Haywards Heath, I stood up in the ring and told the punters I hoped they had enjoyed it, and that they could look forward to a lot more good wrestling the following week, as other promoters had booked the following fighters . . . Just how simple can you get? While I was giving the others a plug, some people seemed to be busy trying to pull out mine.

Every time J.J. or I went to book a hall it seemed that the council entertainments officer would lock himself in his office and send a clerk to fob us off. When we started asking questions, we found out that there were rumours that we were heavy villains who had to be watched, as we were likely to rearrange the faces of those who didn't do what we wanted. It took us some time to kill the story. When I finally got some good halls on the books, and the entertainment managers were happy with the quality and production of my shows, I used them as references when I came across managers I had to convince. 'You know so-and-so,' I'd say. 'Ring him up. He'll tell you what we are like.'

Then it appeared there was a problem with the printer who did my show bills. Now this printer specialised in wrestling bills. He had picture blocks of all the lads, and you only had to ring him up, tell him who was fighting, and he'd compose the bill for you, putting in the appropriate pictures of the fighters. Then he said he was sorry, but he couldn't do any more work for me, because if he did he felt he'd lose another very big order. Did I understand? I rather thought I did. So now I had to train another printer.

When I rented private halls, I'd turn up on the night with the wrestlers, and in a corner perhaps I'd find a roll of show bills which had cost me fifty quid to print. Somehow they hadn't gone up, so the town's punters didn't even know the show was on. That kills you. A dead loss.

And the battle of the halls went on. I'd have a great show and a full house at a town and then, when I telephoned a week later to book the same hall again, I'd be told: 'Sorry, but another firm has booked it for a year'. Halls I went after were, it appeared, rented for a year by 'another firm'. I often found that most of my bills in a town had been torn down, or 'cancelled' strips had been stuck across them. If I announced a good bill in a small town, a rival firm might move in a couple of nights before and put on a really big show with all their top names. Sometimes, splitting the available audience, another show would be put on in the same town on the same night. Then nobody would make any money.

Eventually, I did most of my business with councils working on a percentage basis, which was normally 70–30. They provided the premises and I produced the show. The bigger the audience the more money the council got. So they made sure my bills were prominently displayed on the hoardings.

Then I started to be continually outbid. At Great Yarmouth, for instance, the hall owners were offered 35 per cent of the take, instead of the 30 per cent they were getting from me. Things escalated from 30 per cent to 50. This meant the show would only break even if the place was filled every night. Later, however, several big councils came back to me because they knew I pulled more punters by giving better value for money.

I had trouble from other promoters. Normally a wrestler works for the man who books him first. That's the code. So I'd book a wrestler, bill him prominently, and then, on the night, he wouldn't turn up. It seemed that someone else had offered him more money — and a lot of steady work — if he would only appear for them.

Sometimes there were men in my audiences stirring up trouble. They'd shout: 'Rubbish, bloody rubbish,' and so on, then: 'Bring back so-and-so'. If this happened when I was wrestling, I'd take the urine back in a big way. 'If you don't watch out, Big Phoney'll be about,' I'd say, pushing out my stomach and waddling around the groin. Then I'd lay on the floor, kick my legs in the air like a big beatle, and shout: 'Can't get up, can't get up. What do you want, three minutes of this, or shall I try to bump my belly against someone as well?' This usually got a good laugh, and the 'plants' were shouted down.

When I staged a show at Poole, the chairman of the council came to see me before we started and said he had 'received information' that I was using the same wrestlers, with masks, then without them, and if this was true he would be very unhappy because it was deceiving his townsfolk, who were paying very good money. He agreed to stay and watch the show, and when the masked men finished their bout I whipped him off to the dressing room. When they came in, I asked them to de-mask, and when they did he could see, of course, that there had been no doubling up during the night. The chairman nipped off, quite happy and full of apologies. He also said he'd enjoyed himself.

At Grimsby I did some 'fly posting'. Fly posting is when you stick up your posters on hoardings, etc. without getting permission — or paying for the space. An awful lot of people do it. Anyway, I was staging this show at Grimsby, and others were putting on a show at Cleethorpes, just a cough and a spit away. So, to put us in with a chance, J.J. and a mate went up to Grimsby for a day, with a couple of buckets of paste and two brushes, and popped up our bills all over the town. Now there had been fly posting in that part of the country for so long, with one poster stuck on top of another, that some wads were inches thick. In comparison, our bills were pretty skimpy.

But blow me if I didn't get a letter from Grimsby Council telling me that if I didn't come and take down all our posters we'd be prosecuted. When we got there, we discovered that the only wrestling posters in the town were ours. Every other bill had been removed, or so it seemed; ours stood out, which tipped off the council.

Promoting, as you can see, is a lot of fun. But, as everybody kept telling me, 'that's business'. Even some wrestlers got me at it, because in the beginning I was the prize green berk of the year.

They used to charge me £5, £8, £10 travelling money, and I'd dish out the cash like a Scotsman with no hands, never bothering to check, only to find later — when somebody got Brahms and talkative — that they'd been diddling me. One bunch of wrestlers I booked told me that they were coming by car, and I said that's fine. Then they telephoned to say the car was up the creek and I said, all right, you'll have to use the train. I met them at the station, and I paid their fares (you have to pay for accommodation, too) which made them very happy. Particularly as they'd all come down by car, sharing the petrol money, and then gone to the station, where they'd bought platform tickets and kept out of sight until they could join the crowd leaving the appropriate train. But once they'd had too many bevies, somebody opened his mouth, and the words got back to me. And I learned. Did I learn!

At Ramsgate, a bloke pleaded with me to put him on first so that he could get home to his poor old mum, who was very poorly, and I wiped the tears from my eyes and said all right. When the bell went I had a stroll around the hall, and I'd hardly had time to get to the front of the building when the bastard disappeared. Two rounds and off with a screech of tyres. He'd done a double, hadn't he? Nipped straight from my show to one in Sheerness, where he picked up another wage packet. A little bird told me. He never worked for me again. A Japanese wrestler pulled the same stunt on me, saying what terrible trouble he was having with his wife, and he was the *main event*. May his ancestors punish him.

But the biggest laugh of my sucker days was when 18 wrestlers turned up to fight on my bill at Clacton, and the surplus geezers convinced me that I must have mistakenly double booked. Without a blink, I paid them all, one lot for performing, one lot just for coming. Conned again. The word went out: 'If you've got no work, just go down and see old Pallo. He'll pay you when you get there.'

It all cost me a lot of money, but oh, I learned all right, and quite a few of the clever bastards found out that old Pallo could pull a stroke or two himself. It didn't take me long to discover which wrestlers were passing on information about my bookings, plans, etc. So, over the months, I arranged to provide a lot of false details. For example, I'd let it be known that I'd done my market research on some hick town, at the back end of nowhere, and that they were all mad keen on wrestling and were begging me to put on a show there. The walls would be bursting with punters. I would be quids in. I'd name the hall and the date, and lo, the same hall would be booked for a show three days before mine was due, and bills announcing an all-star cast. Dear oh dear. A lot of money was lost.

Apart from all this carry on, there was the additional aggro caused by some cowboys who did a lot of rubbishing in the name of wrestling, especially in small venues. They'd book a hall, then saturate the place with posters carrying pictures, say, of McManus and myself (or maybe Steve Logan and Steve Vidor) and a supporting cast of Fred Smurf, Dr Carbuncle, Joe Bloggs and the Left-Handed Frogman, or whatever. But there was a get-out phrase on the poster which said: 'Among the wrestlers invited to appear are . . . ' Of course, on the night, when the hall was nicely full, the cowboy would announce regretfully that although me and Mick been invited to appear, we couldn't because of a car accident, bubonic plague, or any such nonsense. However, at the last moment, the equally famous Red Cloud and Black Mamba had stepped into the breach to entertain them together with

Fred Smurf and co. There'd be some moaning, but most of the punters would stay on to see the rubbish. One bloke told me to my face that he'd made an awful lot of money out of me *not* wrestling for him. I believed him.

There were also more unscrupulous cowboys, who used famous names, took advance bookings, then did a runner. So you will understand the difficulties I had when I wanted to stage one of my own shows in one of the venues that had been conned in this fashion. 'Oh yes,' the punters would say, 'but Billy Muggins Promotions told us you were going to wrestle here three months ago and you never turned up. Why should we believe you now?'

Nevertheless, I progressed. I managed to take over a great many summer venues, and these shows were very successful for a time. Then they faded. Probably the most profitable was the Isle of Wight, where I ran the wrestling for eight years.

Unfortunately, I allowed my setbacks to make me very angry indeed, and this affected my judgement and caused me to make many mistakes. You see, the first show in any particular hall should indicate to the promoter whether it is going to be worth his while to continue to stage wrestling there. Several times I realised that a venue was no good for me, but then I heard that someone else was after the hall, and, because I was angry, and stubborn, I decided to give it another try, then another. So I lost money. Hitchin, Barnsley and Sheffield were three typical examples.

At first, I was charging the punters 75p and £1, but I eventually managed to up the price to £2, but that was not enough to keep up with inflation and, in the end, the percentage I was getting was not a sufficiently big earner. I might make more than a grand on one show, then lose it all on the next three, and, looking back I now realise (when it's too late) that I would have been far wiser to run two good bills a week, rather than present seven or eight, but I needed to keep wrestlers in work if they were to stay with me.

To keep the costs down, J.J. and me wrestled on our own bills, both singly and in tag, sometimes up to seven times a week. 'Hey ref, you won't get paid Friday if you don't let them win,' the punters would shout. But, for the first three years, we lost far more often than we won, which established that the man who pays the piper doesn't always call the tune. But it didn't work out. I was to discover that the punters really wanted us to win.

When I first started I talked to a lot of wrestlers and let it be known that I would pay well and that I would look after them as best I could. 'You're a freelance if you work for me,' I'd explain. 'You can work for anyone else you want. I'm taking a gamble. It's up to you if you want to take a chance as well.' There was a reasonable amount of good young talent around, and I was paying anything from £8 a bout upwards, with the bigger draws getting £50, £60, even a ton a fight. Some of the top men worked for me — Les Kellett, Ricki Starr, Johnny Kwango, Adrian Street, Tony and Iggy Borg, the Maltese boys, Johnny Kincaid, and then I was joined by good workers like Ray Crawley, Neil Sands, John Kenny, Monty Swan, Al McKay, Dave George and Ken Knight. I broke into the market, despite the lure of television, and in six years I was working at least half the country's 350 wrestlers.

At the beginning, J.J. decided on a new image, called himself Solitaire, pretended to be an expert in Kung Fu, and wore a white outfit, including a mask. But Solitaire only lasted around a month because the lad didn't like the mask. He felt he couldn't establish himself as a character if people couldn't see his facial expressions. So he reverted to Jackie Pallo Junior. At the same time, he was doing a tremendous amount of work helping to establish the business.

One of my better decisions was to ask Max Crabtree to matchmake for me. I liked Max, and I'd known him for a long time. A good ex-wrestler, he'd done some promoting on his own in Scotland, and also worked alongside de Relwyskow and Green. Max was good. He had to be to make a star out of his brother, Shirley, also known as Big Daddy, who doesn't seem actually to wrestle at all though he has a fair knowledge of the game.

Max had asked me to go into promoting with him in 1965, but at that time I decided I owed loyalty to Dale Martin. Now

I was returning the compliment. Max was doing really good work, and to keep him happy, I even agreed to him putting brother Shirley on the bill a few times. Shirley too had told me he was keen to try his hand at promoting, just before I left Dale Martin.

Also, after I had been on my own for several years, Johnny Dale came to see me at my home, in Minster, Kent, and asked if he could come in with me as a partner. It was Johnny and Jackie Dale, an ex-wrestler, who founded Dale Martin with Les Martin, a commercial artist, in the mid-40s, and before the takeover, he was its managing director. Now, under his brother Billy, he was overshadowed, gradually losing interest. I told Johnny I'd be happy and proud to have him join me but, tragically, he was taken ill before we could take the deal any further, and soon afterwards he died.

Max Crabtree left me abruptly when he was made a generous offer to matchmake for Joint Promotions, with a view to running the whole outfit in the future — the job he now does.

I also had a top-class show cancelled which I had arranged to stage on Clapham Common. At the last minute, somebody complained to the Lord's Day Observance Society that it was wrong I should be allowed to desecrate Sunday in such a manner, and the law stepped in.

Billy Dale invited me to lunch, and wondered if there was any way we could get back together, or do things in conjunction. He asked me why his brother John had come to see me, and I told him. He wasn't pleased. However, he was very friendly, even when I told him there was no way I would come back to Joint, but that I would listen to an offer if he wanted to buy me out. He was still smiling when we said goodbye.

I would have won if I had managed to get a slice of the television contract for Pallo Enterprises in 1982 when the contract with Joint Promotions ended its five-year run and came up for grabs. We put in a very professional presentation, saying that we only wanted to put on six shows a year, initially, so that the network, and the punters, would have an opportunity to compare our promotions with those of Joint. After all, in the world of *real* sport, like boxing, viewers get plenty of chance to compare different promotions. So why not in wrestling, particularly as it was shown under the banner of 'World of Sport'?

I argued that wrestling was being damaged by the inferior fare being shown to the viewers, and that I was willing to take a chance to prove it. I was confident that we could dramatically improve the viewing figures, and pointed out that it was no good arguing that seven or eight million people still tuned in every Saturday, as the same number of people were watching 20 years ago, when there were three times fewer television sets.

We got very close. Word trickled back that several of the big advertisers on the wrestling spot were in favour of my idea, but as the thing chuntered on, the World Cup contract, representing umpteen million viewers all over the globe, came up for negotiation, and our little grunt and groan contract got pushed into a siding. In the end, Joint got it again. They'd been staging the fights for over 20 years and the attitude seemed to be that it was better the devil you know.

Pity, because my bills were excellent. Many wrestlers working for others were disgruntled because they were treated like small boys: 'Be naughty, and you won't appear on the box'. Also, they were only paid £40 a fight when they did. They get around £60 now, but only because I put the word around the network. And that's still silly money when you consider that actors get more than that for a walk on part saying two words.

Mind you, if I hadn't been so green when I started out, I may have got a piece of the contract when it first came up for renewal in 1977. I'd met John Bromley, who runs ITV sport, at a Water Rats do, and he told me he was concerned that so many of the top faces were missing from the box, and that he'd like to talk to me about it. We arranged to meet for lunch in the Wig and Pen Club, at the top of Fleet Street, London, and, of course, I should have employed some top-liners to draw up a presentation (as I eventually did), and come along with J.J.

and me. John Bromley turned up with a couple of high-powered executives who wanted to know all about the wrestling scene, and we arrived armed only with half a dozen bills of shows we were running. We gave them the rundown all right, but we were not equipped to talk and negotiate at their level.

I kept plugging, writing letters to the heads of all the network companies involved and some of them even wrote back agreeing with me. In the meantime, I also phoned Cliff Morgan, the BBC's head of sport, a very nice bloke who said sorry, but the company wasn't interested.

But who knows? Other channels are opening up. And in a few years' time the ITV contract comes up for grabs again . . .

TEN PLENTY OF SEATS – NOT ENOUGH ARSES

The standard of wrestling staged for television today is such that it seems to be killing the game in the halls and the home. What used to be an entertaining 'sporting' spectacular, backed by professionalism, has been degraded to near farce, destroying what image the business once had. So the ratings are dropping.

All right, so some six million may still switch on come Saturday to watch the antics on the screen. But how many of them would go out on a cold night — or even a warm one — to watch the same stuff in their local hall? Not a lot. Personally, I'd rather watch Batman and Robin, as many of the performers are so inept it looks as though the promoter might as well have gone out into the street, pulled in the first good-looking teenager who passed by, then told him: 'Here, put on these trunks and this pair of boots. Right, now you're a TV star.'

There was a time when everybody who came into the game had to be pretty tasty, but only about 15 per cent of the lads about now could deal with an out of order drunk. The rest are excellent at dressing up silly, screaming, shouting, jumping about and general verbals, just as I was, but when the banter and rucking was over I worked, I grafted. Some modern wrestlers spend so much time on the floor I sometimes think they've gone to sleep, so do many of the punters.

Which brings me to Big Daddy and Giant Haystacks. To recap, Big Daddy is the brother of Max Crabtree, who runs Joint Promotions for Billy Dale. His real name is Shirley, and he told me he was named for Shirley Temple, a little girl his mother liked a lot in films. There the resemblance ends. There is another brother, Brian Crabtree, who is frequently seen on television as a Master of Ceremonies and referee, and he completes the Crabtree wrestling family. Statistics vary, but Shirley is said to be 6ft. 2in. tall, weighting 24 stone, while Haystacks, an ex-Manchester car dealer, is quoted at 6ft. 11in. and 31 stone. Shirley used to wrestle as the Fighting

Guardsman, sporting a bloody big busby, and, in 1974, I gave each of them £10 to fight for me at Slough, but only because Max said they badly needed the money. They were disappointing then, and they are no better now. If anything, they now get out of breath more quickly.

Don't get me wrong. I don't dislike Shirley or Max. In fact, Max stuck out his neck for me once, I'm told, saying it would be a good idea if his company made peace with Pallo. He didn't get far. They're nice blokes. It is just the way the business is going that troubles me, and many other wrestlers, too.

Now I can't remember whether Big Daddy has lost during the past nine years. Certainly he hasn't lost on the box, and Haystacks, naturally, loses *only* to Big Daddy on the box. Fine. It's the old gee-up stuff. The eternal challenge. The I-hate-you-and-just-wait-and-see-what-I'm-going-to-do-to-you-next-time bit. Just like me and McManus used to do. Nothing wrong either with the ballyhoo and razzmatazz, the girls, the bagpipes, little kiddies being patted on the head, scowling and gnashing of teeth. All good stuff. The problem comes when the timekeeper finally rings the bell for the first round, because very often it is the last round, too.

A few years ago I watched the big Big Daddy v. Haystacks fight at Wembley. Thousands were spent advertising it, I'm told, and £48,000 was taken in the box office. Ding went the bell, and one and a half minutes later — just ninety seconds — after three sneers and a few belly butts, Haystacks went over the top rope. That was it. And it seems to be like that nearly every time. Occasionally you might get a few more minutes and a belly flop thrown in, but nothing to satisfy even the most gullible punter. Mind you, some believe it, because there's nowt so queer as folk. But the real punters simply yawn.

One television critic has said it was good material for a Whitehall farce. If he'd written that only eleven years ago, the wrestlers would have been up in arms. Now they just shrug their shoulders and *agree*, and that's not good. Once, they dragged in some 26 stone geezer to 'fight' Shirley. Well, this character thought that Half Nelson was the name of a pub. I recall him walking around Shirley twice and doing the usual hands, knees, and boomps-a-belly, after which he gratefully gave in. Compared with him, Shirley was Jack Pye. This kind of opposition wouldn't have got into a dressing room a decade ago. Now such characters are being billed as TV 'Stars'.

Unfortunately, all the experienced characters who used to be around to tell the beginners where they are going wrong, have disappeared. There are no Lou Marcos to say: 'That was fucking terrible. Now I'll tell you . . .'

A lot of wrestlers wouldn't mind losing to Daddy, Haystacks and company, if they seemed prepared to graft for 25 to 30 minutes and didn't appear to risk heart attacks simply climbing through the ropes. Men like Mighty John Quinn, Eric Taylor, John 'Killer' Kowalski, Kendo Nagasaki could probably have beaten either of them with one hand. But those who complain may jeopardise their chance to appear on the magic lantern and, ironically, although television is killing the game, only the box keeps its pulse beating weakly in the halls.

For the wrestlers who appear on the box on a particular week will pull reasonable houses in the halls for a couple of shows. Then interest wanes again. It's a bit like being bitten by a snake, then being kept alive with an injection of its venom. However, many wrestlers perform to nearly empty houses.

The impact on the game would not have been so dramatic if the top ten wrestlers regularly appearing on television were first-class grafters. Because there *are* good wrestlers to be seen on TV. Men like Dave Finlay, for instance, an ex-amateur champion who started off working with me. He's married to Paula Valdez, a former girl wrestler. Rocco and Jim Breaks are fine performers. So is Johnny Saint. And look at Pat Roach, a good, hard man who couldn't get enough decent fights here. Certainly he has proved he can act. He was excellent in the television series 'Auf Wiedersehen Pet'.

And that's another thing. The good faces are far from happy at getting less than £100 per TV appearance when Joint Promotions are believed to be getting £15,000 for staging each

45-minute Saturday spot. I can tell you, from my own experience, that each presentation is unlikely to cost much more than a grand, and that leaves a more than satisfactorily high margin of profit.

Wrestlers like the Gregories, Steve Logan, Steve Haggerty, Roy Clair, Adrian Street, Al Hayes, Ted Heath, Tony Charles and Billy Robinson have all cleared out. Quite a few are doing very nicely in America. Gone are the larger-than-life men who don't walk wiggly-wobbly. Like Andy Robbins, the great showman who wrestled with Hercules, the brown bear. A real scatterbrain, but a lovely man. 'Come on, Dad,' he'd whisper to me, 'come a little closer. I won't hurt you.' Then he'd nearly pull my head off. But I liked him. Andy was enormously strong. He'd heft a gigantic lorry wheel into the air, and then hurl it across the ring. Once he missed me by about half an inch. Muscular punters would shout: 'Easy, I can do that,' and Andy would challenge them to put their biceps where their mouth was. Of course, they didn't know the bleeding great wheel was filled with weights, did they? Oh shame and humiliation. I couldn't even shift the thing.

But I think there's another contributory reason to the decline in the game, and that is that television and film directors no longer leave anything to the punter's imagination. Let me explain. When I first came into wrestling, and for some time afterwards, it meant something if blood was spilt by the two men in the ring. When I bent a man's arm, I could see, from the faces of the punters that they were bending it with me. Their faces would contort, and they'd be wide-eyed with hate, or adoration, according to their fancy, screaming and waving their arms. 'Twist his arm, break his nose, poke his eyes out,' they'd holler, and they'd go away feeling purified because the lads in the ring had provided an outlet for the aggression they feared to show themselves.

We were for real to them then, like boxers, and we provided the sort of 'reality' they wouldn't find on their television screens, or in the cinema, where cowboys fought each other for five minutes, crashing from balconies, breaking chairs over each other's heads, smashing through windows — and then walked off, without a mark on them. And if a man got shot, he merely clutched his chest and fell over, or off his horse, or whatever. If you were lucky, he'd have a round dot on the middle of his forehead with a tiny trickle of blood coming from it.

Then things changed. When men fought each other on celluloid, they now tended to fall apart, got arms ripped off and ended up covered with claret. And when a man was shot a torrent of blood gushed from the gaping hole in his chest as he was hurled backwards. All very realistic, and, in comparison, pro wrestling was not all that violent, was it? So the punters started to stay at home and watch *The Karate Chop Murders*, or suchlike, instead. Or perhaps they hired a video nasty. You get my drift? Freud Pallo speaks again.

As attendances dropped off, promoters tried everything to revive the public interest. Big faces, like me, were rushed around all over the country to try and fill halls. I was matched against tasty heavyweights, who would win, of course, as nobody was going to believe I could beat somebody half as big as me again. But a lot were curious enough to come along and find out for themselves. I had a good bout with Mike Marino, but pulled only 127 punters against Steve Vidor at Great Yarmouth in mid-winter.

At St George's Hall, Bradford, I fought a challenge match against a *very* big heavyweight named Geoff Portz, who was treated like an emperor up there, while I was the man they most loved to hate. Compared to Geoff I was Tom Thumb, and I'd have needed a brace of .45s to beat him. But it was good fun and put arses on seats. However, the day after the fight, the dustman knocked at Geoff's door and asked: 'How did you get on against that bastard Pallo? You win?' Well, when I saw Geoff he was ranting. 'How dare anyone ask?' he bellowed. 'Don't they all know I could fucking well kill you? Bloody pygmy.'

As if that wasn't enough, I was then matched against John and Peter Cortez, at Rochester, in a 'Two Against One' bout. Both good wrestlers, they ran me off my feet, but the crowd appreciated the performance so much they started throwing money into the ring; the nobbins came to about £12 apiece.

Tag wrestling was introduced to boost attendances, and for some time was very successful. Team wrestling, with four men to a team, was tried too, and gimmicks like 'King of the Ring', and 'Ladder Matches'. In 'King' eight men wrestled each other at the same time, and continued until one ended up the overall winner. In Ladder Matches, a ladder was tied to the ring post, and a bundle of notes — about £250 — was tied to its top. Four men then fought each other, the idea being that the first man to get to the top of the ladder could collar the money and keep it.

Tony St Clair was fighting in one of these frolics one night, and as he got to the top of the ladder, one of the other blokes shook it violently, and the money fluttered down into the audience. Well, it was like throwing a side of beef to piranha fish. There was a bloody great flurry, and in no time half the punters were back in their seats, panting, mopping the sweat from their foreheads, and smiling. The wrestlers were laughing like hell.

When things got a bit more desperate, the business bought Jimmy Savile and Harvey Smith, the horseman. Jimmy is a strong, game fellow, but he doesn't know much about wrestling in my opinion and the rest of the lads, knowing that he was earning many times their money, naturally gave him a hard time. I tagged with him for four or five bouts, and I remember sitting on the top rope, at Nottingham, while Alan Dennison and Sid Cooper whacked him about something awful. I said, 'Come on, Jim, before they bloody well kill you'. The audience fell about.

As for Harvey, he was a hard, strong fellow who'd done a little amateur wrestling. I fought him at Blackburn, and my plan was for me to kick him in the stomach and then, as he bent forward, I'd jump on his back, take his arms, and get a submission. Unfortunately, Harvey was already beginning to bend before I threw my kick. As a result, I kicked him in the eye. It was a poxy bout, but a lovely black eye. The last I saw of him he was holding ice on it. Harvey had thighs like a boa constrictor. When he put the scissors on me he nearly had me in half. 'Harvey,' I hissed, 'I'm not a fucking horse.' He smiled. I liked him. My type of bloke.

One of my gimmicks, when I was promoting, was to put on eight masked fighters, and the punters had to try to guess who they were. As they were beaten, each man de-masked, and money changed hands amongst the punters. And in the 70s, when business was very bad, I brought on the dancing girls. At least, they may as well have been dancing girls, because they certainly couldn't wrestle and were a pain, always wanting to be picked up here and dropped off there.

I was at Dundee, where they had girls on the bill, when this Australian bird persuaded me to give them a try. There were Lolita Loren, Blackfoot Sue, Cheetah, Sue Sexton, Lina Blair, Cherokee Princess, Barbarella, and Mitzi Mueller, who was about the best performer. And maybe one or two I've missed. Some of them were wrestlers' daughters, and I paid them between £18 to £20 a fight.

The girls had been draws, but by the time I got around to using them — as an extra bout — they weren't pulling enough punters. Only a couple of them were attractive, and there aren't enough dirty old men around to fill the halls. Genuine and 'straight' punters tended to dislike them.

Most of them came from Manchester, and I brought them down 13 weeks on the trot, paying their fares and accommodation. On the last Friday, I didn't have a show, but one girl said: 'That's nothing to do with me. I'm here to wrestle, so I want paying anyway.' I paid. But I never worked the girls again.

Today, I'm not working any wrestlers. Like many another good actor, I'm 'resting'. For the last nine years I've fought to establish myself as a wrestling promoter who believed in reviving the old time quality of the game. I've lost. I was beaten by lack of sufficient capital. And don't tell me that money talks. It doesn't. It bloody well bellows.

Professional wrestling has been my life, and I've loved all of it. For 35 years I've done my best to put arses on seats. Now I'm easing my own onto one for a while.

But soon I'll have two completely new hips. And then, you'll be hearing from me . . .

INDEX

Aeroplane Spin 24
Aladdin 95
Andrews, Eamonn 42, 104–6
Arm Jerks 26
Armstrong, Dave 68
Arnold House School 63
Arrol, Don 88
Asseratti, Bert 18, 25, 69–70, 75
Astair, Jarvis 102
'Auf Wiedersehen Pet' 120
'Avengers, The' 95

Back Arm Submission 27
Backbreaker 25
Baldwin, Ernie 17, 68
Barbarella 124
Beaumont, Cliff 17, 23, 73, 92
Beresford, Ted 91, 102
Best, Billy 91, 102
Big Daddy 22–3, 31, 113, 118–20
Blackfoot Sue 124
Blackman, Honor 95
Blair, Lina 124
Blair, Lionel 97
Board of Control 91
Body Slam 25, 26
Body Checks 26
Borg, Iggy 113
Borg, Tony 113
Borienko, Yuri 48
Boston Crab 25, 76
Boswell, Eve 64
Boundy, George 66
Boy Scouts 65
Braden, Bernard 103
Breaks, Jim 120
Brittain, Len 73, 81
Bromley, John 115, 116
Bunny girls 97

Capelli, Eddie 35, 51, 74, 83
Carnera, Primo 61
Carr, Tiny 37

Charles, Tony 121
Cheetah 124
Cherokee Princess 124
Cinderella 95
Clair, Roy 121
Cockburn, Peter 88
Cohen, John E. 88
Colbeck, Alan 20, 24
College Boy 73
Cooper, Sid 123
Cortez, John 122
Cortez, Peter 122
Cottle, Gerry 98
Cowdrey, Colin 97
Crabtree, Brian 118
Crabtree, Max 30, 91, 102, 113, 114, 118
Crabtree, Shirley 31, 113, 114, 118–20
Crawley, Ray 113
Criss Cross Quiz 23
Cross Country 23
Cunningham, Jack 28, 83
Cusick, Jack 83
Czeslaw, Johnny 24

Dale, Billy 91, 102, 103, 105, 114
Dale, Jackie 45, 67, 81, 91, 94, 100, 114
Dale, Johnny 42, 91, 114
Dale Martin 30, 35, 42, 43, 71, 75, 77, 82, 91, 92, 102, 103, 104, 113–14
Dartmoor Prison 97
de Relwyskow, George 91, 102, 113
Dempsey, Jack 17
Dennison, Alan 27, 28, 93, 123
d'Orazio, Joe 37

'Emergency Ward 10' 94
Equity 91–2
Evening News 96

125

Faulkner, Vic 20, 30, 47–8
Fighting Guardsman, the 118–19
Figure Fours 26
Finch, Albert 61
Finlay, Dave 120
Flying Head Mare 23, 24, 28
Flying Head Scissors 23
Flying Tackles 26
Forearm Smashes 24

Gang Show 65
George, Dave 113
Giant Haystacks 23, 99, 118–20
Ginsberg, Abe 30
Godfather 107–16
Goldilocks and the Three Bears 64, 95
Grapevine 23
Green, Arthur 91, 102, 113
Green, Hughie 90
Gregories 121
Gregson, John 93
Grommet 31
Gutteridge, Annie 63–4
Gutteridge, Arthur 61–2
Gutteridge, Dick 61, 65
Gutteridge, Jack, Senior 61–3, 70

Half Nelson 119
Hayes, Judo Al 28, 29, 121
Head Butts 26
Head Drops 27
Heath, Ted 121
Hercules the bear 121
Hill, Joe 37
Horne, Lena 38
Howlett, Chopper 68
Hughes, Frankie 29–30
Hunter, Ray 28, 29
Hutton, Barbara 88
Hutton, Sir Len 97

Indian Death Lock 23
Irish Whip 23, 90
Irvin, Don 65

Johnson, Banger 68
Johnson, Black Butcher 68

Joint Promotions 90–1, 102, 114, 120–1
Joyce, Billy 17
Judd, Mike 103, 105

karate chops 24
Keenan, Peter 30–1
Kellett, Les 18–19, 32, 113
Kenny, John 113
Kidd, George 19, 23–4, 53
Kincaid, Johnny 113
King, Sammy 82
King of the Ring 123
Knight, Ken 113
Kowalski, John 'Killer' 120
Kwango, Johnny 68, 89, 113

Ladder Matches 123
Langford-Holt, Sir John 91
Lincoln, Paul 90, 102, 103
Logan, Steve 16, 20, 101, 111, 121
Loren, Lolita 124
Lynch, Tom 88

Macdonald, Aimi 97
McKay, Al 113
Mackenzie, George 67
McManus, Mick 15–16, 20, 42–5, 47, 93, 96, 101, 102, 103, 104, 111, 119
Mancelli, Tony 68, 79–80
Mann, Tommy 57
Mansfield, Bert 68
Mantoupolos, Vassily 95
Marco, Lou 34–7, 37, 78, 82–3, 120
Marino, Mike 19, 30, 78–9, 92, 101, 122
Martin, Les 75, 87, 89, 91
Maskell, Charlie 75
Maxine, Brian 17, 40
Monkey Climb 23
Morgan, Cliff 116
Morrell, Norman 91, 102
Mr TV 18, 40, 43, 86–106, 96
Mueller, Mitzi 124
Murrant, Jean 57–8
Murray, Bernard 100

INDEX

Nagasaki, Kendo 31, 94, 101, 120
Not Now Darling 103

O'Brien, Archie 29
O'Connor, Des 96
Office Hold 14–15

Pallo, Frank 61
Pallo, Jackie, Junior 30–31, 44–5, 53, 54, 56, 71, 92, 96, 97, 99, 100, 101–2, 103, 104–6, 107, 110, 112, 113, 115–6
Pallo, Trixie 55, 57, 59, 66–7, 70, 77, 86, 87, 93, 96, 97
Pallo Enterprises 105, 114–6
Palmer, Bobby 37, 74
pantomime 64, 92, 95
Parnell, Val 88
Peake, George 34, 36–7, 57
Peter and the Wolf 95
Peters, Johnny 35, 74, 83
Philip, Duke of Edinburgh 89
Pitman, Percy 78, 83
Porridge 97
Port, Geoff 122
Postings 25–6
Preston, Peter 31
Prokofiev, Sergei 95
Purvey, Chick 20
Pye, Dirty Jack 69–70, 75, 120
Pye, Jack 120

Quinn, Mighty John 120

Rann, Peter 82
Reed, Les 96
Rhodes, Joan 87, 89–90
Ring Rats 58
Rix, Brian 100
Roach, Pat 120
Robbins, Andy 121
Robinson, Billy 17–18, 121
Rocco 120
Royal, Bert 20, 21, 23, 30

Saint, Johnny 120
St Clair, Tony 48, 123
Sands, Eric 17

Sands, Neil 113
Sargent, Sir Malcolm 95
Savile, Jimmy 123
Sears Holdings 102
Selvo, Pat 50
Sewell, George 'Chuck' 90
Sexton, Sue 124
shoot moves 22
Shortarm Scissors 26
Simms, Chopper 68
Smith, Harvey 123–4
Solitaire 113
Spain 93–4
Starr, Ricki 24, 45, 113
Stepover Toehold 26
Stone, Stan 74, 83–4
Street, Adrian 101, 105, 113, 121
Swan, Monty 113
Szakacs, Tibor 18–19, 24, 35, 101

Taylor, Eric 17, 40, 120
'This Is Your Life' 104–6
Thomas, Clayton 32
Thompson, Bill 61
Trueman, Freddie 97

Unwin, Freddie 77

Valdez, Paula 120
van Dutch, Izzy 79
Variety Artistes Federation 91
Victory Roll 26
Vidor, Steve 20, 101, 111, 122

Wall, Max 37
Walton, Kent 21, 25, 26, 37, 92
Warwick, John 95
William Hill Group 102
Williams, Johnny 78, 83
Wilson, Bob 62
Windsor, Barbara 103
Witchy Poo 54–5
working moves 22–8
'World of Sport' 12, 115
Wright, Arthur 91, 100
Wryton Promotions 30, 91, 102

Young Atlas 73